SOCIAL SKILLS

THE MODERN SKILL FOR SUCCESS, FUN, AND HAPPINESS OUT OF LIFE

GABRIEL ANGELO

3/16 8/15
LAD
TC 11

5/19
LAD: 11/18
TC: 29

3/13 12/14
LAD
TC 9

302
ANG

CONTENTS

Part I

UNDERSTANDING SOCIAL SKILLS

Chapter 1

THE NEED TO BE SOCIAL

Simply put, humans are social creatures. Most human activity takes place in groups: living, education, worship, playing, even eating. Numerous studies have shown that human health and life span are often dependent on the degree to which a person is sociable. Happy people who interact frequently with others have less disease and live longer than those who socialize less and spend more time alone. [i] In essence, the greatest guarantee of a long and healthy life may be the connections we have with other people.

Early in the history of man, survival depended on the protection of tribes and families. Isolation often meant death; socialization was one of the fundamental keys to survival. Today, being part of a group or community gives us a sense of identity and belonging. It helps validate who we are and is a source of direct help in times of trouble. In short, our connections to other people are indispensable to who we are and how we feel about ourselves. [ii]

The social world we live in today is highly evolved. Being social means living in companionship with others in a community. Today, technology has developed to the point where we carry personal accessories like smart phones that keep us in touch with each other constantly through talk, texting and photos. The internet and sites like Facebook allow people to relay news about everything from major milestones in life, such as births, deaths, and engagements, to something as simple as the mood someone is in or what he is making for dinner tonight. Even more to the point, he can make dinner and immediately post a picture of it along with the recipe.

The biggest change that technology has brought to today's social world is the "instantness" of news. No longer do the discoveries of Columbus take months or years to reach every corner of the world. Today Christopher Columbus would simply Tweet that the world is round, and within seconds the widespread fear of sailing off the edge of the world would be completely eliminated. This recent modern development is profound, and vastly increases our ability to be connected to each other and expand our social quotient. The pros and cons of that immediacy is a separate matter that will no doubt be debated for decades to come.

****

Every day, 200,000 more people join the world's population, which has increased nearly fourfold in the past one hundred years. Demographic data projects that by 2024 the population of the United States will reach almost 335 million people. Sixty percent of the population growth by the year 2050 is expected to occur in China, India and Southeast Asia. Overall, however, Africa's populated is projected to grow 70% faster than Asia's. In sub-Saharan Africa, the population is expected to increase from 770 million to nearly 1.7 billion by 2050. [i]

Growth is expected to be the largest in the least developed countries of the words, which are expected to double in size. This is due in large part to lower levels of education in general and higher infant mortality rates. Less developed countries have a high percentage of youth, where 43% of the population is under the age of 27. In the least developed countries, 40% of the population is under the age of 15, and this poses tremendous challenges in terms of providing education and jobs to a large segment that will be demanding these societal requisites at the same general time. At a time of slow global economic recovery, the needs of these countries to develop a strategy to address the needs of education and creation of employment for its people are critical. At the same time, the number of aged people in the world is expected to triple by 2100. In less developed countries, this will result in a 20% increase in the number of aged people who will need to be supported by the younger generations. [ii, iii]

Currently the world is undergoing the largest episode of urban growth in its history. For the first time, more than half of the world population is living in towns and cities, with the highest concentration taking place in Africa and Asia.

In general, urban areas offer favorable settings for social and environmental issues. They also offer better jobs, income, education, health care and other social services, and these are typically delivered more efficiently than in less densely populated areas due to economies of scale and proximity. Fertility rates tend to be lower in urban areas, but the fact that a large section of the urban population is young means that this population segment will continue to grow. [iii]

****

In addition to the global population growing, it is also increasingly mobile. A significant part of the recent growth of the United States' population is attributable to the relocation of portions of Latin American, Asian and Indian peoples to North America. This changes the face of America, or the ongoing "melting pot" which is the steady flow of immigration that the US has seen for more than 150 years. Thus, the US is one of the most culturally diverse countries in the world.

However, diversity changes the shape of our social landscape, which can also result in what is termed "culture shock." Culture shock is the result of coming into contact with customs and ways of thinking, looking and behaving that we are not used to. This can happen when we travel or when we are at home and encounter people newly relocated to our country. We call it shock because it jars us out of what we are accustomed to. However, the U.S. Census statistics of 2000 show that 11% of people living in the U.S. are foreign born and that 18% of households speak a language other than English at home. Symptoms of culture shock include feelings of anxiety and confusion, headache, lethargy, sleep and digestive problems, irritability and loss of appetite. [iv]

However, the two main keys to overcoming culture shock are keeping an open mind and the willingness to learn about cultures we're not familiar with. Well-traveled people will confirm that no matter where people come from, they all want the same things for the most part: security, companionship, happiness, jobs, homes, families and purpose.

Experts recommend that when we encounter people from different cultures we keep an open mind, refrain from judging, be respectful and maintain friendliness. The more we get to know people, the more we discover they are fundamentally not unlike us, and there are wonderful learning opportunities to be had in getting to know them. People from different cultures can teach us many things about families, new foods, ways of interacting with people, religions and basic ways of thinking. When we embrace diversity, we expand our minds. A diversity of ideas and influences to help us grow and learn. Culture diversity teaches people to recognize and respect similarities as well as differences. Regardless of age, people are often intrigued by the similarities and differences among people. In general, when people are able to recognize and respect common traits as well as unique characteristics, they are better equipped to live cohesively with individuals who are different. [iv, v]

People who have lived in other countries have sage advice to give the rest of us, including the fact that there is no right or wrong—there is only different. They urge us to try to remain continually open-minded, embrace a new way of doing things; try not to resist or judge it. Whenever possible, socialize with people from other cultures. This is a time when people relax and enjoy themselves, it's easier to learn and let down our guard at times like these.

We are all social creatures. As our world grows and changes, we will be required to grow and change with it. The more we understand our social natures, the better equipped we will be to implement **social skills** and acquire new ones.

Chapter 2

WHAT ARE SOCIAL SKILLS?

Social skills are the tools, mechanisms and mannerisms we use to communicate and interact with each other, both verbally and non-verbally, through gestures, body language and in our personal appearance. Humans are social animals, and use a variety of ways to communicate with each other through message, thoughts and feelings with others. When people speak to each other, the message itself can be influenced by verbal language as well as tone of voice, the words we choose to use, and how loudly we speak. We need to be aware how the messages we convey are perceived by the person or people on the receiving end. [vi]

Here are 10 social skills that are considered to be essential basics for everyone, starting when we're very young:

1. **Listen to others**. A big part of socializing is simple listening. Most people enjoy hearing themselves talk, and if you just give them a sympathetic ear, and inset an

occasional comment or related question, you're doing your part in being a good social communicator.

2. **Follow the rules.** We learn this rule very well in grade school. Following the rules keeps things moving smoothly in most situations. Without rules, a lot of situation involving the presence of multiple people might devolve into chaos. Think about situations where you wait in line—at a bank, to buy concert tickets, at the supermarket, voting, etc. If people didn't understand and follow established rules, we'd have a mess on our hands almost wherever we went.

3. **Use eye contact.** This rule is important, although not everyone understands how it works. Using eye contact shows another person that we are engaged in what he or she is saying. Looking away indicates we're bored, distracted or just don't care. When engaged in a conversation, making eye contact says, "I'm listening, I understand, I care." It does mean, however, that you have to stare. It's all right to look away occasionally, especially when the other party does. If this principle makes you uncomfortable, just start do it, a little bit. It won't take long before you get the hang of it.

4. **Take turns when you talk**. No one enjoys a conversation that is monopolized by a single person. Always let others have a say. When others speak, conversations usually become more interesting because you hear different viewpoints that often spark a new perspective on whatever topic is being discussed. People who never let others get a word in edgewise often find themselves left out of conversations.

5. **Ignore distractions**. This doesn't work 100% of the time, but in general, when speaking to another person, don't stop to look at someone passing by or listen to something being said on the radio or down the hall. This is impolite and sends a message to the other party that he or she is not very important. However, sometimes distractions get out of hand, through no fault of your own. When this happens, move your conversation to another area, if possible.

6. **Ask for help when you don't understand**. You'd be surprised how often this *doesn't* happen. As humans, we don't like to admit we don't understand something. It makes us feel foolish, and we hate that. To us, it means we're not terribly bright. On the other hand, most people

are more than willing to help, and very often understand that the topic being discussed can be confusing. The majority of people enjoy being in a position of helping others. It's okay to say, "Would you mind explaining that again?" or, "I guess I'm having an off day, but I didn't follow that."

7. **Be considerate of others**. You'll be surprised at the mileage you'll get out of common courtesy. The world is a hectic, stressful place, and whenever you can help out others, you're helping to ease that stress. Sometimes you don't know how much your actions are appreciated, but you always get points for helping out the other guy, and usually the effort costs us little to nothing.

8. **Don't get angry**. This is sometimes difficult. Everyone has a different temperament, so controlling anger can be easier for some more than others. Usually, however, when we let our anger show, we regret it later. The sage old advice about counting to ten is still very good. Ask yourself: how important is this really, in the whole scheme of things? How much does this matter, or, will I care about this tomorrow? Often that helps put things in perspective. Anger can damage relationships more than we realize, and

typically it isn't worth it. If necessary, pour out your anger on paper, then put it aside. Ninety-nine percent of the time, you'll rip up that paper the next day, and be glad that you did.

9. **Be responsible for your behavior.** Like the paragraph above, this isn't always easy, but most people appreciate it when you take responsibility for your actions. When you sincerely apologize, the majority of people will forgive you—and want to do so. If you think you hurt someone's feelings, made a situation worse by something you did, or spoke out of line, remedy the situation as quickly as possible. You can't go back and undo the behavior, but generally you can defuse any bad feelings.

10. **Do nice things for others.** Like #7 above, a little kindness goes a long way. If you can help someone carry a pile of books, or give a sincere compliment, or just hold a door, it's always appreciated and it's also a great ice breaker and often a conversation starter. And again, kindness costs little to nothing on your part. Go for it. Pretty soon you'll be the person everyone refers to as "so nice."

Sound like rules you learned in pre-school? These are more than just social skills; they're life skills—fundamental rules that make navigating through life easier (which of course is another definition of social skills). [vii, viii]

However, the above is not an unabridged list of social skills. The following are important social skills as well: how to start a conversation, how to introduce yourself to a stranger, speaking in public, how to interact in a group of people, how to be diplomatic when making a suggestion, how to greet a casual acquaintance, how to make an introduction, how to conduct an argument in a mature manner, how to convince someone to adopt your way of doing something...clearly the list could go on for pages. Having social skills means knowing how to interact successfully with others.

Educators say that when people increase their social skills, academic learning increases proportionately, not because social skills make them smarter, but because when people know how to interact successfully with each other, problem behaviors are reduced and learning time is maximized. Researchers emphasize that there are three processes that underlie social skills: seeing, thinking, and doing.

The **seeing** process involves noticing the context around a situation and picking up on social cues. It means noticing behavior, how others are reacting and adjusting our own behavior accordingly. Or, if you find yourself in a situation where you're not sure how to act, watching how others behave is likely to give you useful clues for your own behavior. Monitoring the reactions of others can also help change the course of a situation if things aren't going well. Picking up on visual clues is the essence of the seeing process.

The **thinking** process involves interpreting the behavior of others to understand why they're doing what they're doing. This can be easier said than done, because we sometimes interpret behavior in others by our own subjective beliefs or tendencies. Thus, if we tend to be aggressive in certain situations, we may tend to interpret other people's behavior as aggressive, when in fact it may not be.

The **doing** process refers to interacting with people in positive ways. When we interact this way, there is an almost 100% chance that our actions will be more accepted, agreed to and appreciated. This process is very much like what your mother told you about good manners: do the nicest possible thing in the nicest possible way. [ix]

Here are five distinct advantages to having well developed social skills:

Having better relationships, and more of them: Interacting well with other people leads to more relationships. By developing your social skills you become more likeable and people are more interested in you since you are more interested in them. Most people understand that it's difficult to advance in life without interpersonal relationships. Focusing on relationships will help you get a job, get promoted, make new friends, and give you a better outlook on life. Better relationships also help to reduce the negative effects of stress, which is something most people would like to reduce in their lives.

Better communication: Most of us have had experiences where we thought we were communicating effectively, only to find out later that what we thought we communicated was misunderstood. In reality, this happens more often than one would think. Even people with well-developed social skills can fall into this trap—it's as easy sometimes as just being in a hurry. One helpful antidote to being misunderstood is to take the time to plan what you want to say carefully, and then rethink it. Think, too, about the receiver. What type of person is he or she? What is his personality like? Is he easily offended or is he easy-going and not apt to react one way or another to how a message is delivered? It only takes a few seconds to review these points, and sometimes it can make the difference between effective communication and a problem. [x, xi]

Here's an example of misinterpreted communication: A young man and his new girlfriend were discussing some weekend plans. Both of them had busy schedules and had to make sure they could carve out enough time to attend the social event they'd been invited to. The girlfriend mentioned that she had to go to her office briefly on Saturday to finish up a report with a tight deadline, but that she would be free by 3:00. Her boyfriend felt slightly embarrassed when she said this, since she had mentioned it before and he realized he should have remembered it. His response to her comment was, "Oh, obviously." Because they didn't know each other well at that point, the girlfriend interpreted his remark this way, "Of course you have to go to the office, stupid; you've already told me that." On their date Saturday evening, he couldn't figure out why her behavior was cool and distant. Both of them had felt a bit foolish during their earlier conversation, but didn't realize they were both feeling unsure and a little uncomfortable. Their reactions were personal ones, and had they explored them a little further, they might have avoided the misinterpretation.

The lesson in the above example is that we don't always understand where the other person is coming from. It would have helped if the boyfriend had said, "Silly me; I forgot you already told me that." Instead, he felt a little stupid himself. The girlfriend didn't know how to handle the situation—his comment made her angry, but she knew she couldn't say, "Am I too stupid for you?" because it would only make the situation worse. She might have lightened the mood with humor, such as, "Hey, even I have to slave away on the weekend occasionally!" which would likely have revealed the misinterpretation. But they were both dealing with barriers of not understanding each other fully and some self-esteem issues.

Relating well to people and being able to work successfully in groups naturally develops one's communications skills. After all, you cannot have great social skills without good communication skills and being able to convey thoughts and ideas is a critical skill.

Greater efficiency: Some people dread social interactions because they do not wish to spend time with individuals who do not have similar interests and viewpoints, or they simply find it difficult to relate. It is a lot easier to attend a meeting at work or a party in your personal life if you know some of the people who will be there. If you are in a social situation and do not want to spend time with someone because he or she cannot help you with a particular issue, a good set of social skills will allow you to politely indicate that you need to spend time with other people at the gathering. This can be done diplomatically and in a friendly way, and most people will understand and not be offended.

Advancing career goals: Most desirable jobs have a people component to them, and the most lucrative positions often involve a large amount of time spent interacting with employees, colleagues, and even the media. It is rare that an individual can remain isolated in his office and still excel in his job. Most organizations are looking for individuals with a particular tactical skill set: that includes the ability to work well in a team and to influence and motivate people to get things done.

If you feel your social skills are holding you back in career advancement, there are some things you can do to improve your skills and increase your "business value" at work:

Read – Besides what you're reading now, there are plenty of other self-help books out there. The famous and classic one is *How to*

Win Friends and Influence People, by Dale Carnegie. Most people have heard of this book, and some will even roll their eyes, thinking, "Yeah, yeah, I know all about that." But do you really? The book is written in a very friendly, open and casual style, offering timeless pointers for interacting with people. As you might imagine, the tips in this book are applicable to any segment of your life—not just work.

Support Group – These days there's a support group for just about everything. Check your local newspaper—especially the Sunday paper—for upcoming local events. Also check local community centers, civic centers, and social service agencies. If you can find a group of people who, like you, want to improve their social skills, or who suffer from social anxiety or shyness, you'll not only find support, you'll make new friends. There's nothing quite like meeting people who share your same interests or concerns, and who can offer support, advice, or even just a listening ear.

Take a Course – Toastmasters International is an organization that helps overcome their number one fear, public speaking. It is well known and documented that the top fear of people everywhere in the world is speaking in public. Usually this fear even outranks death. At Toastmasters, you'll be in a group of people who will support you and want to help you succeed, because everyone there feels just like you do. There's also a Dale Carnegie 12-week course in public speaking and social communication. Believe it or not, these organizations and courses are fun. Everyone is there for the same purpose, everyone is a little scared, but virtually everyone enjoys himself (really!). The Dale Carnegie course meets locally once a week and typically each member gives a two-minute speech on an assigned topic. There's a lot of laughter and commiseration, and no one is made to feel foolish. At the end of twelve weeks, everyone marvels at how time has flown by.

Greater overall happiness: Getting along and understanding people will help to open personal and career doors. Having the confidence to start a conversation at a work-related conference may lead to a new job offer with a higher salary. A smile and a friendly greeting in a social situation can lead to a conversation and the formation of a friendship.

As you might suspect, social skills and the processes that underlie them are skill sets that we are continually practicing, honing and learning throughout our lives. Like many things in life, just when we think we have something mastered, we're thrown a curve ball. So we assimilate and continue to learn. Practice makes perfect. [xii]

Chapter 3

CAUSES OF POOR SOCIAL SKILLS

Many wonder why some people seem to thrive in social situations, while others seem to be paralyzed. Is it a matter of personal preference? Are people just born with or without social proclivities? Is it genetic, like height and eye color?

Researchers and scientists have actually studied whether the brains of introverted people are different from the brains of extroverts. Famed psychologist Carl Jung was the person who coined the terms "extrovert" and "introvert" in the early twentieth century. He believed that so-called introverts aren't necessarily shy or insecure—nor are extroverts necessarily always outgoing. Jung believed that the difference between the two lies mainly in the fact that introverts become exhausted by social interaction, while extroverts get anxious when left alone. Introverts need solitude in order to recharge, while extroverts draw energy from socializing. This is a substantial difference. [xiii, xiv]

The reality is that most of us exhibit the characteristics of both types at certain times. We all draw energy from others at times, just as we all need to recharge with some alone time every now and then. Interestingly, however, it does appear that there are a few structural features in the brain that correlate with whether a person is relatively introverted, versus extroverted.

A 2012 Harvard study found that people who considered themselves introverts tended to have larger and thicker gray matter in certain areas of the prefrontal cortex, which is a complex part of the brain associated with abstract thought and decision-making. People who considered themselves extroverted tended to have thinner gray matter in those same areas—which hints that introverts devote more neurological resources to abstract thinking, while extroverts devote less—and perhaps act more spontaneously. xv

And a 2013 Cornell University study concurred with the Harvard study. The Cornell study mixed sample of introverts and extroverts, and then randomly split them into two groups. The first group took the ADHD drug Ritalin, while the second group took a placebo. Participants were then showed a number random of videos such as landscape shots and forest scenes.

After three days of video-watching, the drugs were discontinued and the films were shown again, at which time subjects' alertness and reactions were measured. Extroverts who had taken Ritalin were excited by the films even in the absence of the drug.

However, the introverts weren't happier or more alert after the video, regardless of whether they'd taken Ritalin or not. The researchers thought this result was rooted in a crucial difference between the ways introverts and extroverts process feelings of excitement. Extroverts tend to associate feelings of reward with events in their immediate environment, whereas introverts tend to associate them with their inner thoughts—or perhaps interpret external events as anxiety rather than excitement. [xv, xvi]

Personality differences may also have physiological causes. Although no one has been able to measure a difference in reaction time between extroverts and introverts, research has found that an introvert's brain may process stimuli faster than that of an extrovert. In addition, still other studies have discovered that neurons in the brains of both introverts and extroverts may respond differently to neurotransmitter chemicals which have been linked to anxiety disorders.

These results lead scientists to cautiously draw links between personality types and brain structure and function—but they are quick to point out that this research is in what they consider to be the relative dark ages.

****

Why is it that some people seem to lack social skills and social awareness? Sadly, there are almost as many reasons for this as there are days in the year. Here are a few:

- Lack of proper role models

- Poor self-esteem

- Anxiety

- Shyness

- Lack of practice

- Inhibitions

- Low need to socialize/enjoying solitary interests

- High intelligence

- Personality disorders

- Moving frequently in childhood

- Serious/ongoing illnesses in childhood

- Bullying

- Being from a different culture

- Sexual preference

- Standing out physically in some way (very tall/short, overweight or a deformity)

- Being poor

- Mental health issues

- Abuse (physical or emotional)

- Technology (lack of, or too much)

The good news is that social psychologists have an arsenal of techniques to assist people who have weak social skills. Even better, it is never too late to learn. [xvii] There is no such thing as being too old or set in your ways. *Gosh I'm sorry, but once you're 30 research shows you're just too old to learn how to make new friends.* It just never happens. It's never too late to have a successful social life.

The following is a list of social skills that are easily learned:

- The ability to comfortably meet people and make friends

- Being comfortable in different social settings

- Making conversation

- Making a good impression on others

- Understanding and controlling body language

- Managing anxiety in social situations

- Feeling confident

- Having a positive attitude about being in social situations

You can improve your social skills while your core personality remains intact. Here's a good way to think about it: your personality represents who you are. Your social skills represent how you express yourself. In general, if you have more polished social skills you're able to put your best self forward. Your personality and preferences are fairly enduring. Your social skills are things that, once you've acquired them, you can choose to pull out of your hat to use as needed. There are virtually no downsides to learning better social skills, though it does take work.

Some people feel like time has run out to become social when it really hasn't When you're younger you may unconsciously see life in four-year chunks. High school takes four years and you end up thinking that if you don't hit certain social milestones by the end of that time then you've failed. If you go to college, that's another four years or so. If you don't reach your goals by the time you graduate, then you believe you're really a failure. Even after college, you can mark age 25 or 26 as another waypoint, and then 30. But saying you should have done one thing or another by the end of your college years or else your "loser score" worsens is arbitrary. There's not much difference between a 21-year-old college student and 22-year-old graduate.

Also, younger people have a hazy idea of the future, so you may feel an urgency to have certain experiences right away before you run out of time, but nothing happens when you hit that arbitrary age you're dreading. Life keeps going on for decades and decades. At any point you can devote time to catching up socially, after which you can enjoy the remaining years like anyone else can.

****

What is **social psychology**? Social psychology studies people in a social context. It is the study of how and why people think, feel, and do the things they do depending upon the situation they are in. It explains human behavior as an interaction of mental states and social situations, and asks the question why we behave the way we do in the presence of certain circumstance and behaviors. [xvii]

Understanding social psychology helps us to better understand how groups impact our choices and actions. It also allows us to gain a greater appreciation for how our social perceptions affect our interactions with other people. [x] There are some basic aspects of social behavior that play a large role in our actions and how we see ourselves:

- Our interactions serve goals or fulfill needs. People have common goals or needs that include the need for social ties, the desire to understand ourselves and others, the wish to gain or maintain status or protection and the need to attract companions.

- The interaction between the individual and the situation helps determine the outcome. In many instances, people behave differently depending upon the situation. Environmental and situational variables have a strong influence on our behavior.

- People spend a great deal of time thinking about social situations. Our social interactions help form our self-concept and perception. One method of forming self-concept is by imagining how other people see us. Another method is by considering how we compare to other people in our peer group.

- We also analyze and explain the behavior of those around us. One common phenomenon is our tendency to ignore unexpected attributes and look for evidence that confirms our preexisting beliefs about others. This helps simplify our worldview, but it also skews our perception and can contribute to stereotyping.

- We often believe that a person's behavior is a good indicator of their personality. Another influence on our perceptions of other people can be explained when we decide that the actions and behaviors of others correspond to their intentions and personalities. While behavior can be informative, especially when the person's actions are intentional, it can also be misleading. If we have limited interaction with someone, the behavior we see may be atypical or caused by the specific situation rather than by the person's overriding dispositional characteristics.

****

Social psychology explains attitudes as basic expressions of approval or disapproval, likes and dislikes. Examples would include liking a particular flavor of ice cream, being against abortion, or having a preference for a certain political party.

Well known social psychologists Abraham Tesser theorized that strong likes and dislikes are based on our genetic make-up. Tesser believed that people are disposed to hold certain attitudes as a result of inborn physical, and cognitive skills, temperament, and personality traits. Whatever disposition we inherit, our attitudes are often formed as a result of exposure to rewards and punishments, the attitude that our parents and friends, and the social and cultural environment we live in. Obviously, attitudes are formed through the basic process of learning. Studies have shown that people form positive and negative attitudes toward neutral objects that are in linked to emotionally charged stimuli. [xiii]

Social cognition is a growing area of social psychology that studies how people perceive, and remember information about others. Personal perception is the study of how people form impressions of others. The study of how people form beliefs about each other while interacting is known as interpersonal perception. [xviii]

A major research topic in social cognition is **attribution**. Attribution is the explanation we make for people's behavior, either our own behavior or the behavior of others. We generally attribute causes of behavior to controllable or uncontrollable factors. [xix]

Social influence is a broad term given to describe the effects people have on each other. It is seen as a basic value in social psychology. The three main areas of social influence include: *conformity*, *compliance*, and *obedience*. The first major area of social influence is conformity. Conformity is defined as the tendency to act or think like other members of a group. Individual variation among group members plays a key role in the dynamic of how willing people will be to conform. [vi]

The second major area of social influence research is compliance. Compliance refers to any change in behavior that is due to a request or suggestion from another person. The third major form of social influence is obedience; this is a change in behavior that is the result of a direct order or command from another person.

A group can be defined as two or more individuals who are connected to each another by social relationships. Groups tend to interact, influence each other, and share a common identity. [xix]

Groups are important to humans. To a large extent, humans define themselves by the group memberships that form their social identity. The shared social identity of individuals within a group influences intergroup behavior, the way groups behave towards each other and perceive each other. The tendency to define oneself by membership in a group leads to intergroup discrimination, which involves favorable perceptions and behaviors directed towards the in group, but negative perceptions and behaviors directed towards the out group. Groups often moderate and improve decision-making, and are frequently relied upon for these benefits, such as in committees and juries. A number of group biases, however, can interfere with effective decision-making. [vi]

Social psychologists study interactions within groups, and between both groups and individuals.

A major area in the study of people's relations to each other is interpersonal attraction. This refers to all forces that lead people to like each other, establish relationships, and (in some cases) fall in love. Several general principles of attraction have been discovered by social psychologists, but many still continue to experiment and do research to find out more. One of the most important factors in interpersonal attraction is how similar two particular people are. The more similar two people are in general attitudes, backgrounds, environments, worldviews, and other traits, the more probable an attraction is possible. Contrary to popular opinion, opposites do not usually attract. [xx]

Outer Causes for Poor Social Skills:

When we speak of outer causes for poor social skills we are referring to environmental causes, as opposed to a condition within the human biological system. Outer causes include both social conditioning that a person learns from situations he encounters in the world around him—family situations, relationships with friends and the school environment.

Underlying reasons have been mentioned previously, but can include emotional rejection, abuse, lack of good role models, or an unfortunate living or income situation. [vii, ix]

There could also be situations in which an individual (for a variety of reasons) missed the opportunity to be in an environment where socializing occasions were present, and thus the skills were not learned.

One of these environmental causes is related to the circumstances—family and otherwise—that an individual is born into. Growing up in a family where mother and father have an acrimonious relationship and don't communicate well, or perhaps at all, automatically conditions a child to possess less than ideal social skills. Social conditioning begins at birth, if a child is exposed to fighting, few outward expressions of warmth or love or even verbal abuse, social skills will most likely be substandard. On the other hand, the same could be true of a child with a shy personality who grew up in a loving, positive social environment. His personality plays a role in his ability, inclination or interest in interacting with others. He also may just enjoy solitary pursuits, such as reading, or assembling and painting model airplanes.

A child growing up in a low-income family may feel different from her peers because she doesn't have the latest cell phone or can't afford the current popular $100+ pair of sneakers. Television and social media make these things highly visible, more so than in past decades, since advertising is more directed at youth than ever before, and it reaches its targeted audience immediately. Similarly, a child whose family is from a different ethnic group may feel that she isn't able to blend in with her school peers or isn't accepted because she is different. Some children are able to overcome these differences, but others find them to be significant barriers to social acceptance and the development of skills.

Bullying and teasing have always existed to one degree or another, but recently their profile has increased in an ugly way. Again, social media and the internet seem to play a role, but when a child is bullied by others, the social pressure can be extreme and result in serious damage to social ability. In fact, social withdrawal can occur, and in some highly publicized cases, bullied children have taken their own lives. Children who are being teased or bullied may not talk to adults about it. Instead, they tend to keep it to themselves, possibly out of a sense of shame or hopelessness. If there isn't a sympathetic peer in the picture, a child can become even more isolated. There may even be sympathetic peers around the victim, but they don't know how to handle the situation. The social consequences to the victim can be lifelong, resulting in withdrawal or its opposite—the championing of the underdog wherever he or she is found. Thankfully, bullying is becoming more widely recognized and adults in education and counseling are taking active roles in teaching all children about its inappropriateness, how to handle it, and how to recognize it.

Another unique cause that affects social skills is the high level of technology we are all exposed to today. We have electronic information and amusement at our fingertips 24/7. People carry personal devices that deliver music, news, games, messages, entertainment and ongoing communication. This environment of instant access to personal entertainment can serve—oddly—to isolate people. On college campuses today it is not unusual to see students walking with ear buds firmly in their ears for music and eyes fixated on the screens of their smart phones while their fingers are busy texting messages to people anywhere and everywhere. This can occasion worry when they are unwilling to look up from this preoccupation to look before crossing a street. It is not known whether or not they would hear a fire engine if it was coming toward them.

Being physically different from others can also result in the lack of good social skills. [xxi] If a child is markedly taller or shorter than his peers, is noticeably overweight, or is missing a limb or walks with a limp, it can set him apart to the point he doesn't develop social skills at the same rate as his peers. The peers may also not know how to comfortably interact with him, and adults close to the situation, such as teachers, can play a big role in helping everyone to realize that even though people have differences, they also have many similarities, and everyone appreciates kindness and friendliness.

Childhood obesity has taken the spotlight recently in the media, and the multi-pronged awareness campaign in the media, in schools, and to families is having an impact on this difference that may set children apart. In fact, a lack of social skills may be a part of what causes stress overeating that contributes to obesity. In general, the taboos that used to keep topics out of the news are being eliminated. This means that the awareness of childhood obesity, as well as the acceptance of different sexual preferences, are likely to go a long way toward reducing or eliminating the barriers to the development of good social skills that some children encounter. [xxi]

Some of the barriers listed above can result in a child's sense of personal failure or unworthiness—she becomes conditioned to being rejected. For a young person, this can be very difficult to overcome alone, and it may or may not be fully understood.

Here are some positive steps that can be taken to help such a child:

What are the child's interests? A concerned adult in a child's life can usually identify interests or talents the child has, and the child should be directed toward activities that underscore this interest or talent. For example, art classes, music lessons, theater groups, scouting, sports and even volunteer work can all help a child break out of her shell and exposes her to others who will see her skills and learn to like her for who she is without focusing on things that make her different.

Counseling. Talking to an understanding professional may make a difference, and/or participating in some group therapy sessions can help a child put things in perspective. Group sessions also expose her to sympathetic people in similar situations who may become friends sharing a common bond.

Having Fun: Most situations do improve, and until they do, encourage the child to have fun in whatever ways work for her. Let her watch movies, read, go to museums or to the mall; whatever allows her to enjoy herself.

Find a Mentor: Sometimes someone older—a teen or pre-teen perhaps—can act as a mentor to help the child ease into situations that would otherwise be difficult. Even if this person is paid to help, a sympathetic ear or companion can sometimes act as a bridge from an unsuccessful period to a successful one, and be a friend at the same time.

****

Inner Causes for Poor Social Skills:

Social neuroscience is an interdisciplinary field devoted to understanding how biological systems implement social processes and behavior. It uses biological concepts and methods to inform and develop theories of social processes and behavior. Humans are fundamentally a social species, rather than existing as independent individuals. As such, man created organizations beyond the individual—structures that range from families and groups to cities, civilizations, and cultures. These organizations evolved hand in hand with neural and hormonal mechanisms to support them because the consequent social behaviors helped these organisms survive, reproduce, and care for offspring long enough that they too survived to reproduce. [xxii, xxiii]

Traditional neuroscience has for many years considered the nervous system as an isolated entity and largely ignored influences of the social environments in which humans and many animal species live. We now recognize the impact of social structures on the functions of the brain and body. These social factors impact the individual through a continuous interplay of neural, metabolic and immune factors on brain and body, in which the brain is the central regulatory organ. Social neuroscience investigates the biological mechanisms that underlie social processes and behavior which is believed to be one of the major problem areas for the neurosciences in the 21st century. Social neuroscience refines theories of social behavior, and it uses social and behavioral data to advance theories of neural organization and function. [xxii]

Throughout most of the 20th century, social and biological explanations were widely viewed as incompatible. Advances in recent years have led to the development of a new approach drawn from the social and biological sciences. The current field of social neuroscience emphasizes the blended relationship between the different levels of organization, including all known scientific mechanisms to foster understanding of the human mind and behavior.

****

Social Disabilities:

There are three elements of social interaction: *social intake, internal process,* and *social output.* [xii]

Social intake involves noticing and understanding other people's speech, vocal inflection, body language, eye contact, and even cultural behaviors.

Internal process involves interpreting what others communicate to you as well as recognizing and managing your own emotions and reactions.

Social output involves how a person communicates with and reacts to others, through speech, gestures, and body language.

Social interactions require is required interpret, or "read" what other people communicate. Picking up on spoken and unspoken cues is a complex process.

For a child with learning problems, i.e., may misread the meaning or moods of others. There are three potential problem areas for such kids with social disabilities: [vii]

- Inability to read facial expressions or body language

- Misinterpreting the use and meaning of pitch

- Misunderstanding the use of personal space

If a child struggles with these issues, concerned adults should ask if his particular learning difficulty could be causing the problem. Is he inattentive or easily distracted when dealing with others? Does he have a hard time grasping what other people say to him?

Having read another person's social cues, a child has to process the information, extract meaning, make sense of it and decide how to respond effectively. This is an internal process. This ability is called "emotional intelligence," which is a form of social intelligence that involves the ability to monitor feelings and emotions in oneself and others, discriminate among feelings and use this information to guide thinking and action.

If a child misses or misinterprets another person's words, meaning, or mood, he'll end up processing incorrect or incomplete information. This can lead him to inaccurate conclusions and inappropriate reactions. And if a child is impulsive, he may react before processing all the social cues and deciding on an appropriate response.

It can be difficult to observe exactly how one's own child processes social cues internally. But if you are concerned about how a child's internal gears process social data, you might gently probe by asking him how and why he decided to respond to someone in a particular manner.

After a child interprets and internalizes social cues from other people, he then responds. This behavior, social output, is easy to observe. But it can be painful or frustrating to watch if the child's response isn't appropriate.

Inappropriate responses can take many forms. If the child didn't understand a question or comment, his response may seem silly (such as nervous giggling) or unintelligent (an irrelevant answer). Another child may overreact with angry words or actions. Finally, if a child has really tuned out, he might not react at all, even when a response is required or expected from him. Understandably, such responses can cause problems and confusion with family members, friends, classmates, and teachers. [xii, xviii]

This social incompetence creates a person's lack of interpersonal skills with family, friends, acquaintances, and authority figures, such as teachers and coaches. Social competence is necessary for effective interpersonal functioning. They include both verbal and nonverbal behaviors that are socially valued and are likely to elicit a positive response from others.

****

Autism:

One of the most common social disabilities that hamper social competence is **autism.**

Autism spectrum disorder (ASD) is a range of complex neurodevelopment disorders, characterized by social impairments, communication difficulties, and restricted, repetitive, stereotyped patterns of behavior. Autistic disorder, also called autism or classical ASD, is the most severe form of ASD, while other conditions include a milder form known as Asperger Syndrome. [xxiv, xxv]

Although autism varies significantly in character and severity, it occurs in all ethnic and socioeconomic groups and affects every age group. Experts estimate that 1 out of 88 children will have an ASD. Males are four times more likely to have autism than females.

The primary feature of autism is impaired social interaction. As early as infancy, a baby with ASD may be unresponsive to people, or focus intently on one item to the exclusion of others for long periods of time. A child with autism may appear to develop normally and then withdraw and become indifferent to social engagement.

Children with autism may fail to respond to their names and often avoid eye contact with other people. They have difficulty interpreting what others are thinking or feeling because they can't understand social cues, such as tone of voice or facial expressions, and don't watch other people's faces for clues about appropriate behavior. They may also lack empathy. [xxv, xxvi]

Many children with autism engage in repetitive movements such as rocking and twirling, or in self-abusive behavior such as biting or head-banging. They also tend to start speaking later than other children and may refer to themselves by name instead of "I" or "me." Children with autism don't know how to play interactively with other children. Some speak in a sing-song voice about a narrow range of favorite topics, without regard for the interests of the person to whom they are speaking.

Children with the characteristics of autism may have other conditions, including Fragile X syndrome (which causes mental retardation), tuberous sclerosis, epileptic seizures, Tourette syndrome, learning disabilities, and attention deficit disorder.

About 20 to 30 percent of children with autism develop epilepsy by the time they reach adulthood.

ASD varies widely in severity and symptoms and may go unrecognized and therefore not diagnosed, especially in mildly affected children or when it is masked by more serious handicaps. Very early indicators that require evaluation by an expert include:

- no babbling or pointing by age 1
- no single words by 16 months or two-word phrases by age 2
- no response to name
- loss of language or social skills
- poor eye contact
- excessive lining up of toys or objects
- no smiling or social responsiveness.

Later indicators include:

- impaired ability to make friends with peers
- impaired ability to initiate or sustain a conversation with others
- absence or impairment of imaginative and social play
- repetitive, or unusual use of language

- restricted patterns of interest that are abnormal in intensity or focus
- preoccupation with certain objects or subjects
- rigid adherence to specific routines or rituals.

Health care providers will often use a questionnaire or other screening instrument to gather information about a child's development and behavior. Some screening instruments rely solely on parental observations, while others rely on a combination of parent and doctor observations. If screening instruments indicate the possibility of autism, a more comprehensive evaluation is usually scheduled.

A comprehensive evaluation requires a multidisciplinary team, including a psychologist, neurologist, psychiatrist, speech therapist, and other professionals who diagnose children with ASDs. The team members will conduct a thorough neurological assessment and in-depth cognitive and language testing. Because hearing problems can cause behaviors that could be mistaken for autism, children with delayed speech development should also have their hearing tested. [xxv, xxvii]

Children with autistic behaviors but well-developed language skills are often diagnosed with Asperger syndrome. Much rarer are children who may be diagnosed with childhood disintegrative disorder, which is a condition where they develop normally and then suddenly deteriorate between the ages of 3 to 10 years and show marked autistic behaviors. Scientists aren't certain about what causes autism, but it's likely that both genetics and environment play a role. Researchers have identified a number of genes associated with the disorder.

Studies of people with autism have found irregularities in several regions of the brain Other studies suggest that people with autism have abnormal levels of serotonin or other chemicals in the brain. These abnormalities suggest that autism could result from the disruption of normal brain development early in fetal development caused by defects in genes that control brain growth and that regulate how brain cells communicate with each other, possibly due to the influence of environmental factors on gene function. The theory that parental behavior is responsible for autism has long been disproved. [xxv]

Studies strongly suggest that some people have a genetic predisposition to autism. Identical twin studies show that if one twin is affected, there is up to a 90 percent chance the other twin will be affected.

There are a number of studies in progress to determine the specific genetic factors associated with the development of autism. In families with one child with autism, the risk of having a second child with the disorder is about 5 percent. This is greater than the risk for the general population. Researchers are looking for clues about which genes contribute to this increased susceptibility. In some cases, parents and other relatives of a child with autism show mild impairments in social and communicative skills or engage in repetitive behaviors. Evidence also suggests that some emotional disorders, such as bipolar disorder, occur more frequently than average in the families of people with autism. [xxvi]

For many children, symptoms improve with treatment and with age. Children whose language skills regress early in life—before the age of three—appear to have a higher than normal risk of developing epilepsy or seizure-like brain activity. During adolescence, some children with autism may become depressed or experience behavioral problems, and their treatment may need some modification as they transition to adulthood. People with autism usually continue to need services and support as they get older, but many are able to work successfully and live independently or within a supportive environment.

There is no cure for autism, unfortunately. Therapies and behavioral treatments are designed to help specific symptoms and can bring about substantial improvement. The ideal treatment plan coordinates therapies and treatments that meet the specific needs of individual children. Most health care professionals agree that the earlier the intervention, the better.

Educational and behavioral interventions: Therapists use highly structured and intensive skill-oriented training sessions to help children develop social and language skills. Family counseling for the parents and siblings of autistic children often help them cope with the particular challenges of living with an autistic child.

Medications: Doctors may prescribe medications for treatment of specific autism-related symptoms, such as anxiety, depression, or obsessive-compulsive disorder. Antipsychotic medications may be used to treat severe behavioral problems. Seizures can be treated with one or more anticonvulsant drugs. Medication used to treat people with attention deficit disorder can be used effectively to help decrease impulsivity and hyperactivity. [xxvi]

There are a number of controversial therapies or interventions available, but few are supported by scientific studies. Parents are generally warned to use caution before adopting any unproven treatments. Although dietary interventions have been helpful for some children, parents should be careful that their child's nutritional status is carefully followed.

****

Asperger Syndrome (AS) is an autism spectrum disorder (ASD), one of a group of complex neurodevelopment disorders characterized by social impairment, communication difficulties, and restrictive, repetitive patterns of behavior. Other ASDs include autistic disorder, childhood disintegrative disorder, and pervasive developmental disorder not otherwise specified (usually referred to as PDD-NOS). [xxii, xxiv]

ASDs are considered neurodevelopmental disorders and are present from infancy or early childhood. Although early diagnosis using standardized screening by age two is preferred, many with ASD are not detected until later because of limited social demands and support from parents and caregivers in early life.

The severity of communication and behavioral deficits, and the degree of disability, is variable. Some individuals with ASD are severely disabled and require substantial support for basic activities of daily living. Asperger Syndrome is considered by many to be the mildest form of ASD and is synonymous with the most highly functioning people with ASD. [xxiv, xxvii]

Two core features of autism are: a) social and communication deficits and b) fixated interests and repetitive behaviors. The social communication deficits in highly functioning persons with Asperger Syndrome include lack of the normal back and forth conversation, lack of normal eye contact, body language, and facial expression and trouble maintaining relationships.

Fixated interests and repetitive behaviors include repetitive use of objects or phrases, stereotyped movements, and excessive attachment to routines, objects, or interests. People with ASD may also respond to sensory aspects of their environment with unusual indifference or excessive interest.

The prevalence of AS is not well established. It is often not recognized before age five or six because language development is normal until that point. Although ASD varies significantly in character and severity, it occurs in all ethnic and economic groups and affects every age group. Experts estimate that as many as 1 in 88 children will have an autism spectrum disorder. [xxiv] No studies have yet been conducted to determine the incidence of Asperger Syndrome in the adult population, but studies of children with the disorder suggest that their problems with socialization and communication continue into adulthood. Some of these children develop additional psychiatric symptoms and disorders in adolescence and adulthood. Studies of children with Asperger

Syndrome suggest that their problems with socialization and communication continue into adulthood. Some of these children develop additional psychiatric symptoms and disorders in adolescence and adulthood.

Why is it called Asperger Syndrome? In 1944, an Austrian pediatrician named Hans Asperger observed four children in his practice who had difficulty with social integration. Although their intelligence appeared normal, the children lacked nonverbal communication skills, did not demonstrate empathy with their peers, and were physically awkward. Their speech was either disjointed or overly formal, and their all-absorbing interest in a single topic dominated their conversations. Dr. Asperger called the condition "autistic psychopathy" and described it as a personality disorder primarily marked by social isolation. [xxii, xxiv]

Dr. Asperger's observations, published in German, were not widely known until 1981, when an English doctor named Lorna Wing published a series of case studies of children showing similar symptoms, which she called "Asperger's" syndrome. Wing's writings were widely published and disseminated. AS became a distinct disease and diagnosis in 1992, when it was included in the tenth published edition of the World Health Organization's diagnostic manual, *International Classification of Diseases* (ICD-10). [xxiv, xxvii]

Children with Asperger Syndrome may have speech marked by a lack of rhythm, an odd inflection, or a monotone pitch. They often lack the ability to modulate the volume of their voice to match their surroundings. For example, they may have to be reminded to talk softly every time they enter a library or a movie theatre.

Unlike the severe withdrawal from the rest of the world that is characteristic of autism, children with Asperger Syndrome are isolated because of their poor social skills and narrow interests. Children with the disorder will gather enormous amounts of factual information about their favorite subject and will talk incessantly about it, but the conversation may seem like a random collection of facts or statistics, with no point or conclusion. They may approach other people, but make normal conversation difficult by eccentric behaviors or by wanting only to talk about their singular interest. [xxvii]

Many children with AS are highly active in early childhood, but some may not reach milestones as early as other children regarding motor skills such as riding a bike, catching a ball, or climbing on outdoor playground equipment. They are often awkward and poorly coordinated, with a walk that can appear either stilted or bouncy.

Some children with AS may develop anxiety or depression in young adulthood. Other conditions that often co-exist with Asperger syndrome are Attention Deficit Hyperactivity Disorder (ADHD), tic disorders (such as Tourette syndrome), depression, anxiety disorders, and Obsessive Compulsive Disorder (OCD).

The cause of ASD, including Asperger Syndrome, is not known. Current research points to brain abnormalities in Asperger Syndrome. Using advanced brain imaging techniques, scientists have revealed structural and functional differences in specific regions of the brains of children who have Asperger Syndrome versus those who do not have the disorder. These differences may be caused by the abnormal migration of embryonic cells during fetal development that affects brain structure and "wiring" in early childhood and then goes on to affect the neural circuits that control thought and behavior. [xxviii]

For example, one study found a reduction of brain activity in the frontal lobe of children with Asperger Syndrome when they were asked to respond to tasks that required them to use their judgment. Another study found differences in activity when children were asked to respond to facial expressions. A different study investigating brain function in adults with AS revealed abnormal levels of specific proteins that correlate with obsessive and repetitive behaviors. [xxii, xxvii]

Scientists suspect that there are genetic and environmental components to Asperger Syndrome and the other ASDs because of their tendency to run in families and their high level of occurrence in twins. Additional evidence for the link between inherited genetic mutations and AS was observed in the higher incidence of family members who have behavioral symptoms similar to AS but in a more limited form, including slight difficulties with social interaction, language, or reading.

A specific gene for Asperger Syndrome, however, has not been identified. Instead, the most recent research indicates that there are most likely a common group of genes whose variations or deletions make an individual vulnerable to developing ASD. This combination of genetic variations or deletions, in combination with yet unidentified environmental insults, probably determines the severity and symptoms for each individual with Asperger syndrome.

The diagnosis of Asperger Syndrome is complicated by the lack of a standardized diagnostic test. In fact, because there are several screening tests in current use, each with different criteria, and the same child could receive different diagnoses, depending on the screening tool the doctor uses.

Asperger Syndrome, also sometimes called high-functioning autism, is viewed as being on the mild end of the ASD spectrum with symptoms that differ in degree from autistic disorder. Some of the autistic behaviors may be apparent in the first few months of a child's life, or they may not become evident until later. [xxiv]

The diagnosis of Asperger Syndrome and all other autism spectrum disorders is done as part of a two-stage process. The first stage begins with developmental screening during a "well-child" check-up with a family doctor or pediatrician. The second stage is a comprehensive team evaluation to either rule in or rule out AS. This team generally includes a psychologist, neurologist, psychiatrist, speech therapist (as with autism), and additional professionals who have expertise in diagnosing children with AS.

The comprehensive evaluation includes *neurologic and genetic assessment*, with in-depth cognitive and language testing to establish IQ and evaluate psychomotor function, verbal and non-verbal strengths and weaknesses, style of learning, and independent living skills. An assessment of communication strengths and weaknesses includes evaluating non-verbal forms of communication (gaze and gestures), the use of non-literal language (metaphor, irony, absurdities, and humor), patterns of inflection, stress and volume modulation; pragmatics (turn-taking and sensitivity to verbal cues), and the content, clarity, and coherence of conversation. The physician will look at the testing results and combine them with the child's developmental history and current symptoms to make a diagnosis. [xxv]

There is no cure for Asperger Syndrome. The ideal treatment plan coordinates therapies and interventions that meet the specific needs of individual children. There is no single best treatment package for all children with AS, but most health care professionals agree that early intervention is best.

An effective treatment program builds on the child's interests, offers a predictable schedule, teaches tasks as a series of simple steps, actively engages the child's attention in highly structured activities, and provides regular reinforcement of behavior. This kind of program generally includes: [xxii]

- social skills training, a form of group therapy that teaches children with AS the skills they need to interact more successfully with other children

- cognitive behavioral therapy, a type of "talk" therapy that can help the more explosive or anxious children to manage their emotions better and cut back on obsessive interests and repetitive routines

- medication, if necessary, for co-existing conditions such as depression and anxiety

- occupational or physical therapy, for children with sensory integration problems or poor motor coordination

- specialized speech/language therapy, to help children who have trouble with the pragmatics of speech—the give and take of normal conversation

- parent training and support, to teach parents behavioral techniques to use at home.

With effective treatment, children with AS can learn to overcome their disabilities, but they may still find social situations and personal relationships challenging. Many adults with Asperger Syndrome work successfully in mainstream jobs, although they may continue to need encouragement and moral support to maintain an independent life.

The incidence of autism and Asperger Syndrome seems to have increased dramatically in the past decade or so. There is a general feeling that the increased prevalence is likely to be associated with environmental factors. Although communication with these disorders is disturbed, the general population has a higher level of awareness of it, and is in a generally better position to deal with it.

As a population we are being forced to deal with a general lack of social skills on an increasing basis. At the same time we are also adapting to increasing numbers of people from other cultures living among us, which demands that we adapt to changing communications needs as well. Then there is the matter of our high-speed, highly advanced technology, which serves to limits our contact with live human beings.

Keeping up our social skills is a challenge in this environment, but one that we have to meet. As society evolves, we need to accept human behaviors as they are no matter how much we may want things to remain as they used to be. Change is here, and it generally doesn't ask our permission before arriving.

PART II

SOCIAL SKILLS DEVELOPMENT

Chapter 4

Social Developmental Progression

The development of social skills is a never-ending cycle throughout life. Skills we need at one point in life we may not need a decade later. However, as we evolve, so does our need for different social skills.

As children we learn the fundamental rules of getting along with others. We refine these behaviors in our early school years, but may need a different set of skills as teenagers when our bodies and minds are maturing and although we may look like adults, we may be questioning our looks, our confidence and our popularity and actually withdraw socially for a time as we figure out life. As college-aged young adults we may experience our highest level to date of sociability, and these are the years we often meet our future mate. We graduate, get married and get our first "real" jobs.

The workplace brings a new need for the development of more social skills. We spend hours every day in close quarters with people not of our own choosing, and we have to get along. We may be members of work teams for the first time, and perhaps we're exposed—sometimes to our bewilderment—to that ubiquitous animal, office politics, which is a land mine of both danger and opportunity. This is when many people sink or swim with a magic concept known as diplomacy.

As we mature as adults, we may find we have less need for the social dynamics of our teenage years—life is busy and we don't have time for cliques or worrying about who's popular and who's a geek. This is a time when we start our own families and all of a sudden we are the role models for the social skills our children learn. The tables have turned! Now *we* are responsible for someone else's well-being and development. Suddenly, things have gotten very serious.

Literature devotes a great deal of attention to the development of social skills and needs of the baby and growing child, but not as much is devoted to the elderly in our society. Social skills evolve throughout the human life cycle, and the field of geriatrics presents its own set of challenges and required skills.

For instance as Baby Boomers increase in age, the face of the American population will change dramatically. By the year 2030, a projected 71 million Americans will be age 65 or older, an increase of more than 200 percent from the year 2000, according to the U.S. Census Bureau. Researchers estimate that 6,000 people turn age 65 every day and, by 2013, 10,000 people will turn age 65 every day. [ii]

Aging health care consumers will increase the demand for physician services. In the United States, people over the age of 65 visit their doctor an average of eight times a year, compared to the general population's average of five visits per year. [xviii] Doctors will see an increasing number of older patients, and by developing a greater understanding of the aging population and how to enhance communication with them, doctor-patient interactions will be enhanced.

This communication process in general is complex and is further complicated by age. One of the biggest problems physicians face when dealing with older patients is that their wide range of life experiences and cultural backgrounds often influence their willingness and ability to remember and follow doctor's order.

Communication can also be hindered by the normal aging process, which may involve sensory loss, decline in memory, slower processing of information, lessening of power and influence over their own lives, retirement from work, and separation from family and friends. At a time when older patients have the greatest need to communicate with their physicians, life and physiologic changes make it the most difficult. [i]

Because unclear communication can cause the whole medical encounter to fall apart, physicians should pay careful attention to this aspect of their practices.

Chapter 5

DEVELOPING SOCIAL SKILLS IN CHILDREN TO TEEN

As should go without saying, social skills are a critical part of functioning in society. Having good manners, communicating well and being considerate of the feelings of others are all important components of good core social skills.

Now helping kids develop social skills prepares them for a successful life of healthy interactions with the people around them. From the time they are born, there are many things parents can do to help their children develop well socially.

In infancy, babies are only aware of their own needs. When they cry and make noise, respond to them in your own language. This encourages them to attempt to speak. Give lots of attention and love. Kissing and holding babies is important for their development. It is a basic human need and does not spoil a child. Parents should be calm around babies. When you respond to your baby's cries and needs, you're starting to teach him or her to be considerate to the needs of others. Although it may be tempting to panic or express frustration around a crying baby who has kept you up all night, breathe deeply and calm yourself in order to model a harmonious social environment. [xix]

Babies enjoy social interaction, and their smiles and coos demonstrate this.

Use mirrors to allow a baby to look at himself; let him see his expressions. Use his name often when you speak to him—you're encouraging the beginnings of healthy sociability as you allow him to explore and interact with you and the rest of his family. Be your child's best cheerleader. Create a warm, nurturing environment. Talk about yourself and let your child listen and interact to the best of his ability. While still a baby, let your child watch other children play from a distance; this is teaching him the basics of social interaction before he really understands them.

Children in the toddler stage have learned some words and basic sentences. For the most part they play alone and don't understand the concept of sharing yet. Still, parents can help them by creating a social, respectful atmosphere at home. Inviting other parents and children over exposes toddlers to other people, and they begin to learn basic rules about sharing and feelings. They learn to use words to express their feelings, and to be gentle when touching people and pets. Toddlers should be praised and rewarded for positive, cooperative behavior; this is the start of social behavior.

As children grow and become preschoolers, they should be helped to expand their circle of friends. Now that they can talk, they should be encouraged to make friends with other children. Arranging play dates and parties gives a child a broad background against which to enhance her social skills.

Preschoolers are old enough to learn about being sorry, not hitting, and apologizing for their behavior. Words should be emphasized over actions, i.e., it's better to say, "I don't like that," instead of hitting a playmate. Children at this age should learn to talk about their feelings. Parents can ask them to explain how they feel about things they experience, and also help them to find the right words to describe their feelings.

School age children have many built-in opportunities to observe and imitate adults. Good manners are learned and refined at this age. Positive examples include greeting people in a warm, friendly way and speaking respectfully to everyone. This is also when kids begin to learn problem solving techniques. A teacher or parent can intervene in a conflict, encourage the expression of feelings, and ask each child how he's feeling. Let the children make suggestions as to how the problem should be solved. [xii]

This is a good time to teach children to appreciate each other's strengths and differences. Encourage them to praise good qualities and positive performance in others, and help them to understand what those same qualities are in themselves. This is the time in a child's life when he learns about being a friend, how to cooperate and how to share and take turns. The early and middle school years give kids an enormous opportunity to become wonderful social creatures.

Among the many things the school years teach are:

- Being patient; everyone waits to take his turn and everyone gets a turn.
- Participation—joining in even if you're not very good at something.
- Helping out others. Everyone needs to feel cared about.
- Following directions; rules keep everyone safe and well.

- Being focused – getting one's job done and not interrupting others from doing theirs.
- Accepting the differences in people and knowing that everyone in unique and has feelings.
- Learning to be an active listener by using eye contact and paying attention.
- Using praise and not put downs; never being mean.
- Being polite and always saying hello to people you know.
- Using good manners in public.
- Being honest.
- Being respectful of other people and their belongings.
- Working out problems when conflicts arise.
- Using humor.
- Not shouting.
- Accepting differences in people and treating everyone equally.
- Never teasing or bullying.
- Being assertive and standing up for yourself.
- Be willing to learn new skills.
- Try something new even if you're feeling shy.
- Don't give up too easily.
- Work together with people and include everyone in activities.
- Being loyal.

- Keeping your word.
- Stay calm and control anger.
- Learning to compromise.
- Being open-minded to new ideas.
- Learning to forgive.

You can easily see that children have a lot of their plates when it comes to learning social skills. On the other hand, children are fast and flexible when it comes to learning, and learning is a process that begins on the day of their birth. Every day and every year is full of practice. Although everyone learns at a different rate, eventually most children become well-functioning adults with good social skills they will practice for the rest of their lives. [viii, xii, xxi]

Teenage Years

Moving on to adolescence, social relationships are a significant priority for teens. Since adolescence is a period where teens begin to transition away from the family toward independent living, learning appropriate social skills can set up a teenager for success. Additionally, teens with social deficiencies may struggle to form socially beneficial relationships, which may lead to depression, anxiety, low self-esteem and poor school performance. Whether you know a teen who is developmentally on target or an adolescent with mental health issues affecting his social skills, teens may benefit from some at-home interventions.

It's important to model appropriate social behaviors. Parents often serve as the primary model for teens' social skills. Warm and responsive parenting is one of the single most important factors in helping a child develop appropriate social skills. Providing a teen with positive reinforcement, emphasizing her strengths and modeling constructive problem-solving skills, can help teens overcome many social deficiencies. [xxix]

Role play with teens using social scripts can be very effective. When we interact with others in the community, we use social scripts (sets of behaviors that dictate what we say and how we behave in a given situation). If a teen has a social deficiency, he might not understand what social scripts to use. A teen can create role playing scripts that explore what he should do if he meets a new person, wants to apply for a job or order a meal in a restaurant. He can then practice using these scripts at home. Parents can help by pretending to be an employer, and the teen can practice asking for a job application. These scripts can be reinforced by asking him to observe your behaviors in social settings, and then discuss later why you chose your particular set of actions and words.

Playing *"spot the error"* is another good learning exercise. Once a teen understands social scripts, asking him to critique inappropriate social behavior can be an effective way to help him learn expected ways of interacting in common situations. You and another person can role play a common social scene, such as asking for directions, and commit a social faux pas. You would then ask the teen to identify a better way to handle that situation and discuss why this new approach would be more effective.

Some teens with social deficiencies benefit from joining therapy group. As an adjunct to home-based skill-building activities, group therapy can be a powerful tool for teens with social deficiencies. Groups designed for them have two purposes: teaching adolescents appropriate social skills and then giving them the chance to practice these new skills with their peers in a safe environment. Additionally, by working with other teens who have social deficiencies, a teenager can normalize his experience and see that he is not alone in his struggles with appropriate socialization.

With each passing year we expect more complex social skills from teens. Every teen will be confronted with different kinds of peer pressure, the desire to date and form more intimate relationships, as well as the need to interact with adults in different circumstances.

Many parents describe their teens as moving away from them as they grow older, but in fact most teens continue to seek advice from their parents, as well as from helping professionals as they navigate the maze of social expectations:

Anger - Problems with anger management can be very detrimental to a teen's social development. No one likes to be with someone who is angry all of the time, or someone who expresses anger in inappropriate ways. Teenagers have to learn more acceptable ways of working out anger, such as talking with a trusted peer or adult, or working out calm, rational solutions with the person she is having a conflict with.

Anxiety and Shyness - Social anxiety is common among teens but can begin at any age. The social environment in high school can be very intimidating. While shyness is fairly common, teens who are anxious about their social interactions can have problems as they grow older, and the anxiety they experience can make life very hard. [vii, xxx] There are many techniques for dealing with these problems, from self-help books to courses on social interaction to therapy groups and even medication in serious cases.

Apologizing - Apologizing in a sincere and appropriate way is a social skill that is necessary throughout one's lifetime. If not learned in childhood, the lack of this skill may make many relationships unnecessarily difficult. It's not hard to understand that most people appreciate a sincere apology, and with a little practice, it's not hard to do, and many people are pleasantly surprised to learn that the recipient is very willing to forgive.

Appearance - Many children don't realize how much their appearance affects their social acceptance. They may think that wearing the right sneakers or jeans is important to social acceptance, but in fact children judge each other on a much deeper level, paying more attention to what is different about other children than what is the same. Teens who suffer from acne or who feel otherwise different from the mainstream can suffer acutely. Anything that can be done to make teenagers feel more like part of the crowd is generally well worth whatever financial investment is involved.

Teasing - Bullying and teasing can take many forms, but it is always hurtful and sometimes extremely disruptive to a child's development. [ix] While it is present in school children of all ages, bullying and teasing tends to peak during the middle and high school years. Bullying has taken on a higher profile in the past few years as social media has contributed to widespread and mean-spirited bullying that has resulted in loss of life. This should be a zero-tolerance topic that teenagers have to understand is completely unacceptable in any form, and help has to be available for anyone who is on the receiving end of bullying or teasing. [xx]

Classroom Behavior - High school students spend a great deal of their time in school classrooms. They are apt to be judged by their peers according to the way the act in these settings. They should understand that respect for everyone is imperative and that acting out will result in banishment from the classroom.

Compassion and Caring - While some kids seem to be naturally compassionate throughout their development, many others can seem indifferent to their classmates and even mean. These behaviors can become more prevalent with the added social pressures of high school. Teachers and counselors need to consistently emphasize the importance of taking others' feelings into account. The Golden Rule comes into play, and in this age group, most teens are able to envision themselves in an uncaring situation, and imagine how that feels.

Compliments - Giving and receiving compliments can be more difficult for kids than most adults realize. If teens are having difficulty in reading social cues they may find it hard to know when to say the right thing or how to say it. This is an area where scripting can be helpful. Etiquette instruction is also a confidence builder in this area.

Conversation Skills - Carrying on a conversation is like a dance, requiring a good sense of timing and the ability to both lead and follow. If you observe a group of teens in a school cafeteria, you can tell in a minute which kids are more "popular" with their peers, almost all of the time it will be the teens with good conversational skills. There are many ways to learn these skills—videos, books, groups, even summer courses. Good old observation and practice are tools that will stand most people in good stead in this area, too. xviii

Cooperation and Compromise - Cooperation involves listening to what others are saying, understanding the benefits of sharing, and becoming comfortable with taking turns. In many situations, working together means coming up with an acceptable compromise. It means that each party gives a little and also gets a little. Studying the art of negotiation is all about learning to compromise, which is a powerful skill.

Dating - Beginning to date is anxiety-producing for most teenagers, and for the parents of teens as well. High school children must now begin to negotiate relationships with peers as well as members of the opposite sex. Using a progressive approach is often successful, and teens need to understand that there are many types of people in the world, and not all are made for each other. A bit of a thick skin helps in this area, and by all means, if at first you don't succeed, try, try again!

Drugs and Alcohol - Unfortunately drugs and alcohol are an important part of the social interaction for many high school students. For some students, taking drugs and alcohol is part of their social identity. They see these high-risk and illegal activities as a way to gain social acceptance. [xiii, xxi] Education is critical in this area, because sometimes the problem only gets worse when teens go off to college. They need to know the risks and implications of using both drugs and alcohol, and certainly the dangers of mixing the two.

Friendships - There are few things more important in childhood than having good friends. Generally, we expect a child to have had at least one "best friend" by the age of eight or nine, and to have a group of close friends by the age of twelve or thirteen. Every so often a child doesn't have a good friend, and this can be heartbreaking for parents. Children need to be encouraged to explore different interests, and this is the most likely path to friendship. Every so often there is a late bloomer who for whatever reason doesn't acquire friends until later, but the key is not to give up. [xx, xxxi]

Greetings - Greetings are the gateway to every social interaction. Greetings set the stage for interpersonal interaction. When teenagers have difficulty with greetings, they send a message that they could have difficulty in other social situations. With a little luck they have been taught from an early age to greet people they know every time they meet. Greetings can be brief, but a smile and the tone of voice is everything. Even a smile and a thumbs up sign does the trick. The most important thing is to be positive.

Group Behavior - Interacting in a group requires a very different set of social skills than interacting with individuals. From the time they enter school, children spend most of their time in groups of children; in the classroom, in the lunch room, on the sports field. People in groups sometimes become bolder than they would normally be alone. This can lead to behaviors that are outside the norm of what is acceptable. Every individual has to be aware of group dynamics, and has to have the assertiveness to walk away if group behavior is getting out of control. [vi]

Patience - Patience—the ability to delay one's own gratification for the sake of others—is an important part of social success. Adults appreciate patient teens and see them as "well-behaved" and somewhat surprisingly, teens appreciate this virtue as well. Patience almost always serves people better than impatience does, and is certainly more appreciated.

Peer Pressure - The pressure to conform to group expectations is a part of being human. We are social animals, and being accepted by others is an important part of our self-image. But some teenagers are overly concerned with the approval of their peers, even to extent of behaving in ways that they know adults will disapprove of. It's important that children understand from an early age that it is never wrong to act in a way that is being true to oneself. We live in a big world with lots of people in it, and it is okay to say no to pressure do to something you feel uncomfortable about.

Personal Space - Most children intuitively know about personal space, when someone is standing too close, when someone is standing too far away, or when someone is touching them in an uncomfortable way. But some children have difficulty learning the rules of non-verbal behavior, including the rules that govern personal space. Everyone needs to learn this concept, and fortunately there are relatively successful ways to demonstrate this to children who have trouble interpreting non-verbal behavior. The behaviors can be demonstrated on them, which will help them feel the full force of the sensation in a safe environment. [vii, xii]

Public Behavior - Adults are very aware of the different social rules that apply when they are in public or in private, but children often don't see this distinction. Our expectations of how children should behave in public change with years, and public behaviors that might be tolerated when they are younger, become inappropriate or even odd as they become teenagers. This is a problem that age seems to repair, but some teenagers may simply need to hear the repetition of the stern assurance that X behavior is inappropriate in public. [xii, xviii]

Secrets and Lies - Everyone keeps secrets, and nearly every one lies at some time, but how and when kids do this can make a significant difference in the way they are viewed by their peers. The gift of good judgment may seem hard to come by for some, but teenagers should understand that secrets and lies can hurt people, and their sense of consideration and manners must be appealed to. This may take some time, but they have to learn that not everything that is thought must be spoken. This mistake can be successfully resisted.

Self-Worth and Confidence - Preteens and teens must respect themselves before they can begin reaching out to others, encountering new people and situations. Children who feel self-worth and confidence have an easier time making friends, handling conflicts, and resisting negative pressures. In a perfect world, children grow up with a healthy sense of self-esteem and would refrain from doing anything that would diminish their own self-respect. But since we do not live in a perfect world, a healthy sense of their own self-worth needs to be reinforced repeatedly. [xviii]

Sportsmanship - "Being a good sport," is more difficult than many people realize. Of course it involves following the rules of the game, but it also involves following social rules; empathizing with the feelings of others, winning graciously, responding appropriately when someone else wins and more. A sense of perspective comes in handy here, including the fact that a sporting event is not the most important thing in the world, even though we might care a lot about it. The teenager should be coached to compare the loss of a game as being relatively small in comparison, say, to world peace.

Technology - In the last few years, technology has changed the way that children communicate. Technology has also brought on a new set of social rules for children, some of which are obvious and some of which are quite subtle. There is a new sense that it is necessary and good to be in constant communication with one's friends, and a little personal time and space can take a back seat. Even though we call this connectedness, it can lead to isolation. Smart phones and tablets that play a customized music library for which the listener wears a set of personal headphones wherever he or she goes also contributes to this isolation. The rapid communication of important news is good, but nothing can substitute for the one on one contact of healthy human interaction.

Chapter 6

DEVELOPING SOCIAL SKILLS IN ADULTS

As an adult, it can be argued that social skills gets easier the older we get, *and* they become more challenging. When you're younger you just haven't had enough time to develop a range of interests. People more easily fit into stereotypes when they're in high school simply because of they haven't had a chance to move beyond the handful of things they naturally got interested in first.

As people get older they've had the time to pick up additional hobbies and flesh out their personality. They can even accidentally get into pastimes they never would have guessed they'd enjoy one day. Of course, the more interests you have, the easier of a time you'll have relating to people and making conversation with them.

You'll also be able to do more things with your friends (i.e., you can go mountain biking with them, instead of bowing out and telling them you'll only meet them for dinner later).

Many people have personalities, interests, or appearances that go against what society says are the right ones to have. When they're younger they can feel really conflicted about this. Following their natural dispositions seems to make them the happiest, but they may also take society's messages to heart and tell themselves things like, "I'm such a loser for being into Anime. Why can't I just like cars and golf and whatever and be a normal person?" [xviii]

As people age they tend to make peace with the ways that they're different. They learn to be surer of themselves and not be too swayed by what everyone else thinks. They decide there's nothing wrong with being the way they are, and that some people will like it and others won't, and that they can handle that. Some people aren't even that old before they develop this mentality. Practically speaking, this means they act and feel more quietly confident, and they no longer hesitate to seek out the type of social life that works best for them (i.e., only having a few friends, skipping on rowdy parties, not being embarrassed about joining a tabletop gaming club).

This isn't to say that once someone becomes comfortable with themselves they rigidly lock their personality down for all time. You can still be open to changing or developing new facets of yourself. You can still identify traits that you want to improve upon. But you don't beat yourself up just because you want to spend a Saturday morning reading a fantasy novel.

In high school and college you're more restricted in who you can spend time with. When you're younger there's an unwritten expectation that you're going to be friends with people close to your own age. But if someone is twenty eight there's nothing stopping him from hanging out with his 45-year-old co-worker, or the 37-year-old guy they play poker with. It's okay to have a wider range of friends, and once you're out in the world you get exposed to a broader group of people.

Sometimes people will tell you that they don't have a ton of friends because they feel like they just don't have much in common with their similar-age peers. When you get older this doesn't hold you back as much. If you feel like you want to hang around more experienced, mature people, or a very specific variety of person, then you can go find them. [xxxii]

Anyone will seem more awkward and out of place if they're plopped in an environment that's not a good fit for them and doesn't value what they're about. When you're younger you're stuck wherever your parents choose to live. If someone goes to college, they don't always have a lot of options about what school to go to, either.

When people get older and gain more independence and money they get more say about what kind of environment they want to be in. Some people come across as "late bloomers" not because they totally changed, but because they were finally able to put themselves in a situation where their true selves could blossom. They can get out of their small, boring town and move to a new city that's filled with their type of people. They can choose a job that matches their strengths and style of socializing. They may live in an area that's not for them, but buy a car and easily be able to drive somewhere better on the weekends. If they prefer living alone they can afford to get their own place. [vi]

Everyone knows that kids and teenagers can be nasty to each other. This is not to say that adults are never mean-spirited or abusive. They are. They can also be jerks to each other in much more subtle, insidious ways. But in general adults are nicer and more tolerant in the face of social awkwardness.

If a young guy is acting a bit shy, his classmates could very well make fun of him to his face.

An adult is more likely to be polite, patient, understanding, and accommodating. That person may try to subtly include or help someone who's being quiet at a party. Especially in certain workplace environments, people are more well-behaved. Even if an adult is put off by someone who's socially awkward, he's more likely to just bite his tongue and stay out of the person's way, rather than try to make the other person's life miserable.

In a lot of ways, this all creates an atmosphere where it's easier and safer for someone who struggles with social skills to be himself, and to work through their issues. Of course, not everything will be perfect. For example, if a person tries to invite someone out who's not interested, he may still get a polite run around. But at least he can be pretty sure he won't be openly mocked for asking the wrong person to come to an event with them.

This is a bit related to the idea of people not being jerks. When you're in high school a diverse group of people is forced to be in close proximity with each other. Even when you want to tell yourself you shouldn't care what everyone else is doing, you can't help but know anyways, and get pulled into it to a degree. This is less of a problem in college, and it almost totally goes away after that. When you're older you have way more freedom to do your own thing and not get a hard time for it. For one, people can't practically follow what you do. They're also busy with their own lives and have better things to do than worry about how someone else spends their days. [xxxiii]

However, on the *flip-side*, it becomes increasingly harder to meet people as a grown-up adult. Now that's not to say it's impossible to make friends when you're older, but it is a little trickier.

Everyone's heard that it's easier to meet people in high school and college. You spend a good chunk of your day surrounded by hundreds, or thousands, of your peers. You may even live in a building full of them. Once you're out of school you have to work harder to make friends.

This starts to happen at a different age for everyone, but there will be a stage when you notice that the people in your life just don't have as much free time to hang out anymore. They're too busy with their jobs, partners, and families. If you're trying to make new friends, or keep a friendship going, this can really get in the way. [xxx] It's not enough to meet someone you get along with, they also have to have enough breaks in their schedule to hang out with you. Not that easy when they have to work on the house, drive their kids to soccer tournaments, and visit their in-laws every weekend. Not to mention the fact that you may be just as busy with the same kinds of things yourself.

Besides having to compete with people's hectic schedules, a lot of the potential friends you meet when you're a bit older may already have well-established social circles, which gives them little motivation to seek out someone new. You may meet someone you get along with at work, but when they do get time off from their family, they go away for the weekend with a bunch of friends they've known since grad school. It can be really tough to break into a group who have twenty years of shared experiences between them.

In high school and college everyone is obviously at the same school. Many of the people you meet also live fairly close by. At a university it's not hard at all to gather up ten people on a Friday night. When you're older, your friends can be all over the place. One person could live in the suburbs half an hour north of the city. Another could live in a feeder community an hour to the west of it. These little things make it that much harder to organize get-togethers, or to hang out spontaneously.

In general, people are less likely to care what you do when you're older. Sometimes this tactfulness goes a bit too far and can leave older people who still struggle with their social skills really lost and frustrated. A middle-aged person may not have as many problems as they did in college, but still have things they want to work on. However, he can't seem to get anywhere with anyone. He knows he's not having the success he wants. He assumes he must be doing something wrong, but no one will give him any clue about what it may be.

Everyone just seems to quietly exclude him. He tried to invite people out, but is met with walls of friendly, reasonable excuses. There's a social life going on at the office, but he's on the outside looking in. [xxxiv] Other people have their own stuff going on and aren't going to take it upon themselves to try and help him out. Even if he wants some direct feedback, everyone is too nice to offer it. At least in high school someone might get annoyed and tell him, "Ugh, you're so desperate and needy! And you wear the same clothes every day!" That's mean, but at least it's something to go on.

Tips for Adults to Improve their Social Skills:

Approach social occasions with a sense of humor. – Humor goes a long way in smoothing human interactions. Most people appreciate humor. Don't take yourself too seriously, either. If something goes slightly awry, don't worry it to death; learn from it and move forward—with a sense of humor.

Look for people with the same interests. – If you love to play chess, you will automatically have something to talk about with someone else who feels the same way. Look for chess clubs and chess tournaments. Chess players are brainy people—you'll be in seventh heaven talking chess lingo with your fellow fanatics.

Don't fear rejection. – You won't like everyone you meet and vice versa. There's nothing wrong with that. Just remember to use good manner and courtesy, and then move on. Focus your energy on finding people you like, but don't make a big deal about it.

Put things in perspective. If you have some anxiety or fear about social interaction, it helps to put it in perspective. Think of it as one evening out of your life, or two hours at a cocktail party. If you put it in a box, it's much easier to keep it in perspective. It's a time interval for you to practice being nice—and it's not as big a deal as world peace. That should help you keep it in its proper perspective.

Accept every invitation that comes your way. – If you want to increase your social skills, make a point of accepting every social opportunity you are offered. At least for now. Doing so will help you get used to different social situations and meeting new people. You will instinctively know when you're ready to be more selective. (You'll have more friends by then, too.)

Be a copycat. – In grade school it was a bad thing to be a copycat, but not now. Watch other people's social interactions; how they converse, how they mingle and work a room. When you see things you admire, add them to your repertoire, and use anything that works well for you, especially if it makes you more comfortable. Observing how other people do things is a wonderful way to learn.

Chapter 7

OUR SOCIAL CONNECTION

It's a known fact that we need other people in order to be well and thrive. We just feel better when we're around other people. We also need close relationships in order to be happy. Why is that? Why are relationships with others so important to our well-being and happiness?

Relationships create a sense of belonging and safety so that we can explore the world and learn about ourselves. When we feel safe and supported, we don't have to worry about responding to danger or finding our next meal. In short, we're wired to be social. [xv]

Characteristics of Close Relationships:
- The ability to love and be loved
- Mutual understanding
- Caring

- A source of help in times of trouble
- Celebration of good times
- Validation of self-worth
- Security
- A diversity of influences to help us grow and learn
- Fun

Belonging to a group or to a community gives us a sense of identity. It helps us understand that we are part of something larger than ourselves. [xxxv] Studies show that people with strong social connections have less stress-related health problems, lower risk of mental illness, and faster recovery from or illness. Friends and family can also encourage and support us in healthy lifestyle habits, such as regular exercise.

Researchers have found that people are happier when they are with other people, more than when they are alone—and the boost is the same for introverts and extroverts. [xxxvi] They also find that happy people are more pleasant, helpful, and sociable. So being around people makes us feel happier, and when we are happier we are more fun to be around, creating an upward spiral of happiness. [vi, xx]

There may be some people in the world who can get along without anyone else, but not very many. We become depressed without contact with other people. That's one reason solitary confinement is used as a form of punishment and behavior modification in prison systems. Our self-esteem suffers when we're alone. The fact is we are happier and more productive around other people.

Happiness may be surprisingly contagious, too. [xxxii] Studies following thousands of people over 20 years found that happiness benefits other people through three degrees of connection, and that the effects of happiness last for a year. There is a statistical relationship not just between your happiness and your friends' happiness, but between your happiness and your friends' friends' friends' happiness. [xx]

The positive effects from connecting with others last a long time. People have a tendency to quickly adapt to changing circumstances. This is why people who win the lottery, for instance, usually find themselves at the same level of happiness they had before they won. Close relationships, however, may be an exception. In contrast to material goods, we are more likely to continue to want our close relationships, even after we attain them, and to continue to derive positive emotions from them. [xxxvii]

When we experience social pain — a snub, a cruel word — the feeling is as real as physical pain. Languages around the world use pain language to express social pain ("she broke my heart," "he hurt my feelings,") but as it turns out, social pain is real pain. Because of how social pain and pleasure are wired into our operating system, these are motivational ends in and of themselves. We don't focus on being connected solely in order to extract money and other resources from people; being connected, as it turns out, needs no ulterior motive. [vi, xviii]

Research data suggests that we are significantly shaped by our social environment and that we suffer greatly when our social bonds are threatened or severed. When this happens in childhood, it can lead to long-term health and educational problems. We may not like the fact that we are wired such that our well-being depends on our connections with others, but the facts are the facts.

We have a profound proclivity towards trying to understand the thoughts and feelings bouncing around inside the heads of people we interact with, characters on television, and even animated shapes moving around a computer screen. Although we are far from perfect at gleaning the actual mental states of others, the fact that we can do this at all gives us an unparalleled ability to cooperate and collaborate with others – using their goals to help drive our own behavior.

The funny thing is that thinking about others' thoughts doesn't feel particularly different from most kinds of analytical thinking we do. MRI research shows that there are two separate brain regions for social and non-social thinking, and that as one region increases its activity the other tends to quiet down—kind of like a neurological seesaw. Here's the fascinating thing. Whenever we finish doing some kind of non-social thinking, the network for social thinking comes back on like a reflex—almost instantly. [xxx]

Why would the brain be set up to do this? It appears that this reflex prepares us to walk into the next moment of our lives focused on the minds behind the actions that we see from others. We're wired such that the best thing for our brain to do in any spare moment is to get ready to see the world socially. That makes a major statement about the extent to which we are built to be social creatures.

Social psychologists think that the self is a much more social phenomenon then it feels like from the inside. There's a region of the brain called **medial prefrontal cortex** that sits between a person's eyes. This region is activated the more a person is thinking about themselves. It is the region that is most clearly associated with self-processing. If you think about your favorite flavor of ice-cream, precious personal memories, or aspects of your personality (e.g., Are you generous? Are you messy?) you are likely to utilize this brain region. [xxx]

The more active the medial prefrontal region is when someone is trying to persuade you of something (e.g. to wear sunscreen everyday) the more likely you'll be to change your tune and start using sunscreen regularly. In other words, we let in the beliefs of others, under the cover, without us realizing it. This socially-influenced self helps to ensure that we'll have the same kind of beliefs and values as those of the people around us and this is a great catalyst for social harmony.

The most important thing may be to educate our children about what we are learning about the true role of our social nature in our happiness and success in life. Intellectually, we know all about these things, but if we don't learn them as children, they may ever really get into our guts and guide our intuitive decision-making. [vii]

Research on the social brain also leads to direct policy implications for education. The data is clear that children learn better when they "learn in order to teach someone else" than when "they learn in order to take a test." Learning to teach someone else is pro-social and relies on the social networks of the brain. School could be doing much more peer learning, where (for example) a 14-year-who has trouble in school is assigned to teach a 12-year- old. The teacher then becomes a coach helping to teach the 12-year-old, and the 14-year- old will reap the benefits of the pro-social learning. [vi, ix]

Chapter 8

BECOMING SOCIALLY SAVVY

We all know people who have great social skills. They love being around people, they're never at a loss for words, and they certainly never appear to be ill at ease or awkward. We'd love to be that way, *but it just isn't in us*. So do we chalk it up to the fact that the savvy people were born that way and that we—hopefully—have other redeeming qualities we can comfort ourselves with?

The fact is that some people are born with a gregarious nature, but there are plenty of people who have to learn to be comfortable with social skills. We all learn these skills from childhood on, but most of us have to practice them continually to be comfortable with them. It pays to watch, learn and listen to others in social situations. There's a lot we can learn about what to do and what not to do. And then we have to put it into practice. Social psychologists talk about emotional intelligence, which is part of being socially savvy.

Interestingly, the employees at LEGOLAND have a high level of emotional intelligence. Their job is to make everyone feel like their Lego project is great. People with high emotional-intelligence are very good at reading people. [xxxi]

Here are some secrets about the social skills of successful (emotionally intelligent) people:

1. They don't try to fake emotion. Trying to fake that we care simply doesn't work. Most people have heard of the study results about smiling. They show that if we really smile, our eyes wrinkle. If we fake smile, those wrinkles are not there. And people can read that subconsciously. Most of what we read sub-consciously is correct. The bottom line on reading people is that we have had thousands of years to perfect the skill, and we're pretty good at it.

In addition, people who work in customer service on telephones are told to smile when they speak to customers who can't see them, because we sound happier and feel happier when we do so. We can also tell right away how someone feels toward us. Researchers at the University of Toronto found that people judge empathy accurately in just 20 seconds of video without sound. This means we are reading faces. This also means that it's pretty difficult for someone who doesn't feel empathy to feign empathy. [xxxviii]

2. They pay attention to personality types. We know we should make people feel good by recognizing them for their work. But it's actually difficult to know the right way to do that; one way won't work for everyone, and, not surprisingly, it comes down to personality. There are four dominant types of personalities, each motivated primarily by either power, relationships, craftsmanship, or ideals. (Anyone can Google the Meyers-Briggs Personality Test and take the test for free.)

Here are the four personality types and how to inspire them. [xxxviii]

Power - Type-A people. For a job well done, reward this person with public recognition when a task or project is finished. At work, reward the person with visionary, forward-thinking projects.

Relationships - The cheerleader type. This person also wants some sort of public recognition, but it should be fun. And the thank-you speech is really important to this person. At work, reward him with projects that are varied and well defined.

Ideals - The crusaders. This person wants to be rewarded along the way, not just at the end. At work, reward this person as part of his team, not alone. Show faith in his ability to build strong partnerships by giving him more work to leverage that skill.

Craftsmanship - The perfectionists. Reward this person for attention to detail, and do it in a private, one-on-one way. They don't want big fanfare. This person wants acknowledgement that he did a good job by seeing executive management adopt his work as the standard. [xx, xxxviii]

3. They judge themselves on how precisely they give a compliment. Socially successful people might not be in a position to reward someone at their company, but most of us are always in a position to acknowledge the work someone else has done. This information helps us understand who wants acknowledgement for what. And we can mention something to them. This seems subtle, but the difference between high emotional intelligence and merely average is that everyone knows they should give compliments when they can. But not everyone knows who needs what sort of compliment.

4. They know how to make conversation. Think back to the most enjoyable conversations you've ever had. Chances are, those conversations moved smoothly from one speaker to the next, and naturally from one topic to another. There was no sense of "What do I say now?" or "Am I supposed to talk next?" You and the other people in the conversation felt free to enjoy spending time with each other instead of worrying about how to make the conversation work. That magical "something" is called conversation flow. Conversation flow happens when conversation is comfortable, effortless and smooth. It's the way conversations are supposed to work. [vi, xviii]

Sometimes, conversation flow seems to happen automatically. Two people hit it off, and the conversation feels really smooth and comfortable. That's great when it happens, but what do you do when conversations don't flow?

That's where the principle of **invitation and inspiration** comes in. Invitation and inspiration are the key ingredients of smooth, comfortable conversation.

- An **invitation** is when you say something that explicitly lets your partner know it is their turn to speak.

- An **inspiration** is when you say something that makes your partner want to speak unbidden.

Both serve to prompt a response from your conversation partner and keep the conversation flowing. These two ingredients create the sense of conversation flow. Learning how to include them in conversations will invite conversation flow into all interactions.

With practice, most people find that invitation and inspiration enable them to build enjoyable, comfortable conversation in most interactions. No awkward pauses, forced segues, or fake small talk.

Here's an analogy about how invitation and inspiration work:

Imagine that you and your conversation partner are working in a (poorly designed) deli. Half of the ingredients are at one end of the deli counter, and half of the ingredients are at the opposite end. The two of you are going to make a sandwich, so you decide to stand at opposite ends of the counter and slide the sandwich back and forth as you work on it.

Your partner adds some lettuce, then slides it down for you. You add some mayo, then you slide it back so he can add some turkey. Now, let's make the image a little stranger. Let's say that you and your partner are chatting as you work (normal enough), but that the sandwich you are making represents your conversation (not so normal.)

You ask, "How was your weekend?" and slide the sandwich down the counter.

Your partner replies, "Oh, it was great. How was yours?" and slides the sandwich back.

You reply, "It was fine," and try to return the sandwich. The sandwich travels six inches and stops dead.

What happened is that you didn't give your partner a clear invitation or a strong inspiration. Without either of those things, your partner didn't know what to say next and perhaps was unsure if it was his turn to speak. So he didn't respond. The conversation lapsed, and the sandwich stopped sliding.

Remember, an invitation is when you say something that explicitly lets your partner know it is their turn to speak. And an inspiration is when you say something that makes your partner want to speak unbidden. Without an invitation or an inspiration, your partner might not know what to say or whether to respond. That's why you want to be deliberate to offer invitations and inspirations to your partner. [x, xviii]

This involve questions, or open-ended statements that can't be responded to with one or two-word replies. They involve thought and explanation, which serve to keep the conversation flowing. And if you find yourself falling into the trap of asking such a question or getting a dead-end response (it happens!), keep going—don't give up.

"What did you do?" "Who were you with" "What was your favorite part of the museum?"

5. They have adaptive social skills Adaptive skills involved the ability to adjust to another type of behavior or situation. This is often characterized by a kind of behavior that allows a person to change an unconstructive or disruptive social behavior to something more constructive. These behaviors are most often social or personal behaviors. For example, a negative repetitive action like snapping gum or cracking knuckles can be re-focused to something less noticeable or bothersome, such as tapping a foot. A social example would be arriving to take a class you expected to be lecture style, only to find that it's an in-the-round discussion in which everyone is expected to participate. A person with adaptive skills would be able to adjust and participate to the best of his ability.

Adaptive behavior reflects an individual's social and practical competence of daily skills to meet the demands of everyday living. Behaviors change throughout development, across life settings and cultures, depending on what we're faced with. The more flexible and open-minded one is, the more adaptive he can be in his behavior.

6. They have cognitive social skills. Social cognitive theory, used in psychology, education, and communication, says that portions of an individual's learning can be directly related to observing others within the context of social interactions, experiences, and outside media influences. In other words, people do not learn new behaviors solely by trying them and either succeeding or failing, but rather, the survival of humanity is dependent upon repeating the actions of others. This is very true in social situations. The more we watch others interact in conversations, greeting, introductions and public speaking the more we learn about doing them and knowing how to do them. We also watch behaviors and decide which ones will work for us comfortably. We can then put our observations into practice and further hone our social skills. This is a trial and error area, but those with savvy social skills are adept at observing and incorporating what they have learned into their own social repertoire. [ii, xxiii]

7. They have social intelligence. This is that sweet spot where we all want to be. It is the knowing that comes with experience. Social intelligence means knowing both intuitively and from experience what to do in various social situations, and then executing the action(s) with skill and grace. Social intelligence (SI) is the ability to get along well with others, and to get them to cooperate with you. Sometimes referred to simplistically as "people skills," SI includes an awareness of situations and the social dynamics that govern them, and a knowledge of interaction styles and strategies that can help a person achieve his or her objectives in dealing with others. It also involves a certain amount of self-insight and a consciousness of one's own perceptions and reaction patterns, and a certain ability to perceive or read those of another person. [x]

Here's an interesting parting thought on being socially savvy. Sometimes this is less about being brilliant and more about not doing something wrong. If you know the basic rules, and you're able to function in day-to-day social situations, you're a success story. The definition of savvy is "practical understanding"—*Einstein* isn't mentioned anywhere.

PART III

SOCIAL SKILLS

APPLICATION

Chapter 9

SOCIAL COMMUNICATION SKILLS

Communication skills are the key to developing (and keeping!) friendships and to building a strong social support network. They also help you take care of your own needs, while being respectful of the needs of others. People aren't born with good communication skills; like any other skill, they are learned through trial and error and repeated practice.

A social skill is any skill facilitating interaction and communication with others. Social rules and relations are created, communicated, and changed in verbal and nonverbal ways. The process of learning such skills is what we call socialization. [xii, xviii]

Communication is critical to human life because it is the primary way we interact with each other. Communication consists of speaking, gesturing, writing, and drawing—and these are just a handful of broad categories.

In many ways, communication is the equivalent of social skills, because when we are in social situations, everything is communication. However, not everyone is comfortable in social situations, and the art of communicating and socializing is something many of wish we could improve on. The good news is that it's never too late to learn good social skills, and learning/improving doesn't need to be difficult.

Improving social skills is a goal that many people have. Many want to be more comfortable in social settings and enjoy themselves more. You don't study social skills so you can sit in your room alone—you study them so you can go out and be social! But how do you actually make that happen? And what does being social mean, anyway? But let's say you've already studied how to make conversation and you've brushed up on your body language. You may not be perfect, but you're ready to put your social skills to use. If that's you, then becoming more social is easy.

First, realize that there is no one right way to be social. "Being social" for one person will look different than it does for others, and that's okay. One young man may play in a different Dungeons and Dragons game almost every night. Perhaps he dedicates the majority of his social time to these games, but it's a social life that works for him. He gets to spend hours with his friends, doing an activity he enjoys.

He may have a friend who goes out dancing three to four times per week. Most of his social time may be dedicated to making new friends or meeting girls on the dance floor, and that's the social life that works for him. Still another person prefers to bounce between a lot of different social activities–his social calendar is always different week to week. That's the social life that works best for him.

The point is that "being social" doesn't mean that people have to hit the bar scene, or go to parties to find their social rhythm. "Being social" means that they discover what a rich, fulfilling social life looks like for *them*, and then they live that out. [xxxiv] If someone needs a long time to rest between social engagements, being social might mean one social event per week. If he thrives on interaction, being social might mean a new event each day. If John already have a solid group of friends, being social might mean that he spends most of his time with them. Or, it might mean that you split your time between your old friends and opportunities to meet new friends. In any case, it needs to be something that works for YOU.

Of course, someone might not know what a rich, fulfilling social life looks like for himself. And that's okay. Like many other areas of life, being social takes time to figure out. But there's an easy process that can help you through it. First, think about your social goals and contrast them with your previous social experiences. Think through what has worked for you in the past, and what has been flawed in the past that you would like to improve for the future. The goal is not to figure things out completely, but to discover a few possibilities for areas where you can grow your social life.

Second, project what you desire in your communication. This means to try something that is new but achievable. Try for that balance of distant but within view when pondering new ways to be more social. In other words, explore new social opportunities that may be a bit challenging or scary (i.e., "distant") but make sure they are still achievable (i.e., "within view.")

This is a repetitive process. You'll spend some time thinking, which will give you an idea for something new for you to try. That new experience will give you more fuel for thought, and your thinking will in turn lead to new experiences. The cycle keeps repeating, and every time it does, you grow a little closer to a full understanding of what being social looks like for you. So there's no rush. Just commit to a slow and steady thinking and planning socially, and you grow steadily closer to the rich, fulfilling social life you desire.

Here are six activities that you can do to help anyone improve his or her social communication skills. [xxxiii] (This should be fun, and works especially well with children.)

- Good, solid **eye contact** shows others that we are both interested in what they have to say and that we have confidence in our ability to listen. Activity: have a staring contest. This is the ultimate eye contact. Making a contest out of making eye contact is challenging, especially for people with a competitive streak.

- **Reading Faces/Interpreting Emotions** - This skill is important throughout life and at all stages of development. Many misunderstandings arise when the emotions of others are misinterpreted. Sometimes people are confused by what a particular look means. They may easily mistake a look of disappointment and think someone is angry, or they may mistake a nervous expression for a funny one.

- Activity: **Emotion Charades**. Instead of using movie or book titles, use emotions. Write down feeling words on pieces of paper. Take turns picking a slip of paper and then acting out the word written on it. You could substitute written words for pictures showing the emotion. Or, you can draw the emotion rather than act it out like in the game Pictionary. You can make it harder by setting a rule that you cannot draw the emotion using a face. Instead, players have to express the feeling by drawing the body language or aspects of a situation that would lead to that emotion (i.e. for sadness, you can draw someone sitting alone on a bench, or a rainy day, etc.)

- When people have a conversation, they pick a topic to discuss. Each person adds something to the conversation until the conversation has finished or the topic has changed. Sometimes it is hard for people to **stay on topic** and take part in a regular conversation. Here are some activities to help with staying on topic and carrying out a conversation. Activity: Play a game with the alphabet where every letter has to be the beginning of a word in a theme such as garden or restaurant: **A**…asparagus, **B**…beets, **C**…carrots.

- **Improvisational Storytelling:** To do this activity, put pictures of different situations face down on the table. Then players decide together on some story elements must appear in the story (i.e., an arctic wasteland, a lemur, and a fire hydrant). The goal is for the players to take turns making up the narrative, building on each other's ideas and (eventually) making use of all the required story elements. To begin, the first player picks a card, and starts the narrative. He can take the story into any direction he likes, but he must incorporate the emotion depicted on the card. After a minute or two, the next player picks a card and continues the narrative. Players continue to take turns until they have used all the required story elements and reached a satisfying conclusion. This activity builds public and extemporaneous speaking skills, which are key fears for many people.

- **Building Self-Esteem:** Most of us aren't fully aware of the things we do that help others. Here's a wonderful exercise that's best done with groups aged teens and up. In advance of a group gathering, ask every member to write something they like about each of the other group members. The comments are collected and then written or typed up about each individual. Pass these sheets out to the appropriate people at the next group meeting. Typically people are not only surprised, but emotionally moved by what their peers or colleagues like about them. Often they don't realize that some of their qualities are noticed and appreciated by those around them. This exercise is a great self-esteem builder.

Chapter 10

SOCIAL SKILLS FOR PROFESSION

A lot of information is available about the basic social skills students and young adults need to get and keep a job, but what specific skills are employers really looking for these days?

With new innovations and ever-changing technology, the workplace is constantly evolving. Being prepared is always part of the answer for job seekers—not only with basic job skills, but with the newest, current "gotta-have" job skills as well. Here some skills that can ramp up a person's employability quotient. [xxviii]

Great Communication Skills - Good communication is essential for any relationship and is especially important in the workplace. Bosses want to know that their employees are able to both listen to and understand instructions and get their points across to customers and co-workers. Job seekers and employees must listen carefully, ask questions, and be clear in order to portray effective communication skills. Since electronic communication is ubiquitous in the workplace, it is also essential that job seekers hone their writing skills. It is easy to be unclear or create a misunderstanding in a text or an email so it is vital that students learn proper tone when writing. Tone can overshadow everything, but so can spelling errors and poor syntax. Students should be taught that when writing correspondence, they should always re-read everything to avoid any potentially awkward or embarrassing spelling or grammar mishaps. "We apologize for any incontinence we may have caused," might be easy enough to mistype, but sending it off in a business email might not go over so well. (Ironically, the age of electronic communication has also resulted in more people who are unable to write in cursive. Indeed, this is not routinely taught in all schools anymore.)

Presentation - Back in the day, job seekers presented themselves on the day of the interview and that was that. Now, job seekers, whether they are aware of it or not, present themselves way before they ever step foot into the workplace. Hiring managers and HR officials introduce themselves to the "online version" of the job candidate before they actually meet him or her. What they find can determine if the job candidate even gets a chance to interview. Job seekers need to piece together their online identities and make necessary adjustments to ensure they appear professional. They need to be aware that potential employers are not only looking at social networking sites such as Facebook and Twitter but will also conduct an online search and could find any blogs, videos, and posts they are a part of. Once someone finds that he or she is squeaky clean in the eyes of the Internet, he should take the opportunity to build up a representation online. Keeping a professional and informative blog or creating a Linked In profile can speak volumes of his overall skills and create networking opportunities. [xxviii]

Being Flexible - Flexibility has always been an important job skill, however it is especially important in today's ever-changing world that job seekers learn to get out of their comfort zone. New programs, technology and ideas are presented daily and employers want to stay at the forefront of change. It's very important that job seekers and employees be easily able to adapt to new rules and ideas. People need to know that they have to roll with the punches. Procedures change over time. If an employee doesn't keep up, someone will come along who will.

Being Proactive- It's easy for a worker to just go to his place of employment, do his job, go home, and start all over again the next day. Depending on the job, this kind of work ethic may be acceptable if an employee just wants to maintain his work status without the promise of advancement or higher wages. However, if workers want to advance in a career, it is important that they are proactive. Companies and businesses today are constantly looking for new, fresh ideas about how to improve operations or create new initiatives. They want employees who bring something original and exciting to the table. Employers also want employees who will anticipate and understand the needs of the company without having to be told. Workers need to know that if they go the extra mile, they will most likely be rewarded in the end.

Influencing People at Work

People enjoy doing business with people they like. This stands to reason. It's the same principle that comes into play when we hang out with people we like. Taking time to build rapport with co-workers can go a long way toward becoming friends. Ask friendly questions about the kids, the weekend camping trip or the latest NBA basketball draft picks. Small talk like this makes people more likeable, and the more we know about our co-workers, the more we identify with them. [xviii]

Most people say they want to be liked at work, but they will admit they would be better off being respected. Sometimes people assume that being popular means being more influential, but respect is more important. Most people think about how other people see them and then they adapt their message, their delivery and their body language to making other people think well of them, rather than concentrating on the essential message.

Demonstrating leadership is one of the ways to build trust and respect.

It's also important to be clear with yourself and others about what you are trying to achieve. State your message to coworkers concisely so that you do not waste their time. Sometimes under pressure we add a lot of extraneous words, or beat around the bush, which makes us less clear. It's better to just get to the point.

It's also very important to understand the context in which others are working. Being sensitive to the cultural and professional constraints under which people operate will help you to tailor your approach to avoid creating unnecessary obstacles which could get in the way of what you are trying to achieve.

The degree to which you listen to other people will have a significant effect on your power to influence people. [vi, xxxviii] Without listening to our co-workers, it is difficult to match our message with their needs. Listen not just to what is being said, but to what is not being said. Listening attentively will help you to discover what motivates people, and you can then use this information to achieve higher productivity and more satisfied employees.

Doing something helpful for another person will make them much more likely to want to do something for you in return. This is called **reciprocity**. Someone in an IT department at a company would be wise to help out another department if he knows that he's going to need the other department's help in an upcoming project he's planning. In the same vein, when presenting an idea to people, explain what is in it for them, not simply why it is good for you or for the company.

It's important to get the timing right, too. Choose your time and place carefully. Would it be better to talk to someone about a proposed project over a coffee or to arrange a meeting when he might feel less pressured?

Be prepared to give up the glory. It's often easier to get something done if you are not adamant that you need to get the credit for it. Also, don't get emotionally attached to your ideas. This could stop you from being able to critically evaluate ideas offered by others, or to see how a number of different suggestions could be linked together to find an effective solution.

The way you look and act can make a big difference. Delivery is very much tied up with non-verbal communication and style. There is no one style that is appropriate for all occasions. It's possible to adapt your style to suit particular circumstances, but it is not always a good idea. Changing your mode of operation can be confusing if people don't know that you are dedicated to what you're proposing.

It's best to guide, not to dictate or manipulate. Show people where you want them to go, but let them work out the path themselves. Avoid being heavy-handed. If you are directing people, you have to allow them enough freedom to figure out their own process. If you abuse your influence, it might work for a period but it could be short-lived because people will resent the way that you are doing it.

Six Quick Tips to Help You Influence People at Work:

- Reciprocation: People are more likely to help those who help them.

- Commitment/Consistency: The message must be consistent with an existing commitment.

- Authority: People are more willing to take notice of someone with authority or expertise.

- Social validation: People are also more willing to take notice if they see evidence others are, too.

- Scarcity: Holding the key to scarce information or opportunities boosts influence—but this principle can also be misused, so be judicious.

- Liking/friendship: People like to say "yes" to those they like.

Communicating Effectively for Management:

1. Consider the Situation before Taking Any Action - Our emotions may tempt us to make quick decisions based upon superficial evidence which may not reflect the true nature of a given problem. Always take the time to consider any problem or situation from all sides, and take time to cool off, if necessary, before making any decisions. Try to figure out what you would have done in your coworkers' shoes. [x, xxxii]

2. Gather and Confirm Information before Making a Decision – Sometimes we have a tendency to confuse symptoms with disease, and consequently treat the symptom rather than the underlying illness. Technology enables us to capture massive amounts of data and slice and dice it to make it appear any way we want. But remember that data is a representation of the problem, not the problem itself.

3. Focus on Problems, Not Personalities – This is an important point, and is another reason why a manager should take plenty of time when making any decision to ensure that she is not confusing problems and personalities. Try using the "24-Hour Rule" which states: don't send any email, message, letter, memo, or report to others until you've had a day to reflect upon its content and are sure it communicates the facts and the tone you wish.

4. Meet Subordinates Face-to-Face - The meaning and intent of written words without the context of a physical presence can be misunderstood, and can subsequently lead to confusion and conflict. There is no substitute for looking someone in the eye and seeing their reaction to your conversation to clarify content and assure comprehension and agreement. Sometimes managers hide behind memos and notes; however, successful leaders seek personable commitment and build trust and mutual respect. Be physically available and "walk the walk." Let subordinates know you are with them through the good and the bad.

5. Assign Tasks Directly and Clearly - People work best when they know what is expected of them. Good managers identify the goals and measures in simple, understandable terms, assign responsibility clearly, and confirm that the information is understood by those who will carry it out. Good managers follow up and give ongoing input to ensure that each subordinate is on the same page and working toward the same objective.

Managers should remember that no employee takes a job with the expectation that he or she will be overlooked, ignored, or insignificant at work. Employees want to be liked and respected by their peers and proud of their employer. Management's challenge is to maintain and develop the employee's enthusiasm and commitment, even during times of stress. Mistakes are part of growing, and falling short and correcting the course are regular occurrences in business and in life. Dealing with subordinates the way you would wish to be dealt with in a similar situation is the best course any manager can take.

Leadership and Emotional Intelligence in Developing Others

Social skills are used when participating in relationships with others. They offer a means of interacting with others that help boost productivity, improve relationships, and increase your general quality of life. People who have high levels of this skill are easy to talk to, make great team players, are good at resolving disputes and are skilled at building relationships. This combination of qualities equates to emotional intelligence.

One of the best indicators of emotional intelligence is the willingness and ability of a leader to help develop others. This type of leader recognizes that helping others achieve their goals is a win-win situation, because doing so also furthers his own development. [x] He is confident enough in his own abilities that he is not threatened by the success of others. When everyone is successful, a sense of connectedness and teamwork is created.

Managers skilled in conflict management are able to recognize that conflict can be an opportunity. It can help coworkers or groups to solve problems, improve processes and learn new skills. Disagreements can be overcome and relationships can be strengthened.

Of course, managing conflict requires a high level of emotional intelligence. A manager must be able to discover the root of the conflict, which may appear, for example, to be about writing a new ad, but may actually be about different parties feeling that their input has not been valued. The manager has to be able to understand the perspective of the involved parties and to help them understand each other. He must be able to manage communication in a way that is positive and productive, and at the same time fosters win-win solutions.

Improving emotional intelligence naturally enhances a manager's ability to build bonds, because his people skills, communications skills and self-confidence will all be enhanced. [x], [viii] But if he focuses on building bonds, he will be creating a type of social network that will increase both the number and type of relationships that he is able to create.

Managers with high emotional intelligence make good friends at work, cultivate networks of professional contacts and friends, spend time developing strong work relationships, keep others informed, and always work on building rapport. Anyone who builds these skills will start to see relationships as bonds that can be proactively built. All relationships will have better quality, too, if the manager's other emotional intelligence skills continue to be practiced.

This type of manager views teams as something that need to be nurtured in order to function at their best. He also understands that collaboration is a powerful tool for decision making, relationship building and creating a productive work environment. This type of emotionally intelligent manager remembers to:

- focus on relationships as well as on tasks

- shares information and resources to foster collaboration

- promotes a climate of friendship and cooperation

- finds ways for all members of the team to bring their strengths to the table

- fosters team identity and pride

- seeks opportunities to build the team's abilities

In short, a leader with emotional intelligence understands that his job is to build people and make them successful, not just himself. When a win-win situation is maintained in the workplace, optimal chances are created for high productivity and worker satisfaction.

Chapter 11

SOCIAL SKILLS FOR EVERYDAY LIFE

Good social skills are important in every segment of life, whether it is relatively formal like school or work, or informal like shopping at the supermarket or shopping with friends. No matter the situation, we have to know how to respond and interact.

Perhaps while grocery shopping you turn down an aisle and come face to face with someone you had a falling out with a few years ago—what do you do?

You might dislike public speaking, and therefore have a singular dread of being called on in class. Or it could be something as simple as wanting to meet a new soulmate, and wanting to brush up on your social skills to increase the chances of that happening in your life.

No matter the reason, it's always a good idea to improve your social skills, and there many resources available to help you. For example, if you would like to make yourself more friendly and social—spending more time with other people and enjoying it—you can do so without changing your personality, and by just making a few adjustments in the way you do things. [xi]

Here are a few pointers (and, by the way, people should only do things that appeal to them and that don't make them uncomfortable). [ix]

Start conversations with new people - If you've recently been introduced to someone, or you see some new people around, go up to them and start a conversation. Even saying hi, asking for their name, and saying, "Cool, nice meeting you. I'll see you around later, hopefully," is fine.

Chat back to people who try to talk to you - Have you ever tried making pleasant conversation with someone you've run into, and they blew you off by giving one-word responses and looking like they didn't want to be spoken to? You probably walked away thinking they were pretty unfriendly, even if you intellectually knew they may have had a reason for being brusque. If someone is trying to chat with you, make an effort to give them something back in return.

Take time to talk to people you already know - If you see someone you know, go over and find out what's going on with her. Keep in touch with your friends. Stop and chat with your co-workers when they're not too busy. Maintain your relationships and show you're interested in other people. If you see someone you know, don't avoid her because you don't feel like talking, or pretend not to notice them because you're worried the conversation will be stilted. Go up to her and chit chat for a few minutes.

Invite people to do things with you/the group - Be fairly loose and generous with your invitations to people. Be the one to invite people out rather than waiting for them to come to you first. Don't feel you have to know someone for a long time, either. If you seem to get along then why not ask them to do something? If you like your new co-worker or classmate, ask her if she wants to grab a drink later, or come by your place to hang out. If you run into a friend downtown, and neither of you is doing anything, ask if she wants to grab a bite to eat, or if one of you is busy, suggest you get together later sometime.

If everyone at work is going out on Friday evening, then ask anyone who may not know everyone else if she wants to come along as well. If you're meeting some friends later that night, ask your new acquaintance if she wants to join you. If you run into a classmate on the street for five seconds, tell her that you're going to be at Dan's place later if she wants to drop by. Of course, when you throw invitations out like this, they won't always be accepted, but that's all right; the important thing is that you make the effort to include others.

Make an effort to bring new people into the fold and make them feel included - If you're out with your longtime friends and there's a new person there, take the time to talk to her a bit, rather than being more aloof and expecting her to make the effort of getting to know you. At the end of the night mention, for example, that everyone is seeing a certain concert in two weeks and invite her to come. If there's a new person at work, fill her in on the general goings on of the office, and let her know everyone in your department usually grabs lunch together at 12:30. Mention that you and three other people usually play football on Thursday evenings if she wants to join in.

Go to where the people are - If you're at work and everyone is going out for lunch then go with them. If they all eat lunch at a certain time and place, then eat lunch then too. If you're at a party and everyone is talking on the front porch, go join them. If you're at a bar and everyone is hanging around on the couches downstairs, then you may as well be there too. Show that you want to spend time with the people you came with. And once you're there, join in whatever they're doing. Don't hang back and focus on something else.

Spend more time with people - Spend time with people more often. Spend longer periods of time with them. Spend time with more of them. If when you normally see your friends, you leave after a few hours, try spending half the day with them. If you only see your friends once a week, try seeing them more often, if they're willing and not too busy. If you usually keep to yourself at work, and only talk to people on break, try spending time with your co-workers a little more during the workday. If you only see some acquaintances of yours under specific circumstances (i.e., in a particular class, at a club), then try to see them outside of that situation.

Make nice little gestures towards other people - Bring food or drinks to a party when it wasn't expected that you do so. Perform basic courtesies like holding doors for people. Buy someone a drink if you're out at a bar. However, less is more. If you're overly nice and giving, you can be taken for granted, taken advantage of, or come across as if you're trying too hard to please everyone and make them like you. It also puts other people in an awkward situation because they feel uncomfortable taking so many free handouts.

Offer compliments to people - Don't be afraid to be positive and encouraging. If someone is good at something, then tell him so. If someone looks nice, or is well dressed, then say you think so. If you think someone is funny, or an interesting person, then let him know. Again, moderation is essential. The occasional genuine compliment is much better than a constant stream of trying-too-hard ones.

Make sure everyone is having a good time when you're out - Without overdoing it and being a pest, put some energy into making sure everyone is having fun when you're out in a group. If someone seems left out of the conversation, try to maneuver it to a topic he can contribute to. Or if someone seems like he wants to say something, but he can't get a word into a lively discussion, casually indicate to everyone that he wants to talk. If you're all doing an activity that someone doesn't seem comfortable with, try to coax him to join in (if it's harmless and you know he'll have fun once he starts), or take some time to explain the basics if he isn't familiar with how to do it. Or maybe help form an alternative side activity.

Shyness and Social Anxiety

There are many people who want to become more sociable and increase their social IQ, but they're shy or have genuine social anxiety. These are bona fide social problems that need to be worked on, but there are solutions, and there are many people who are accomplished "socializers" today because they took the time to overcome their fears.

Many people will say their main social problem is shyness. It's a concept that encompasses a number of sub-issues. In general, **shyness** can include the following: [xvi, xxxix]

Behavior:

- Being hesitant or inhibited in certain social situations.

- Coming across as meek and soft-spoken. Avoiding certain social situations, either entirely or by being in them but not fully participating.

- Being less likely to take social risks. This could be for small actions, like speaking up to tell an edgy joke in a group of friends, or something bigger, like asking someone out.

- Having trouble with self-disclosure.

- Having trouble with self-assertion.

- On occasion, being extra talkative or outgoing (this happens due to nerves, or because the shy person feels she has to act this way because that's what other people expect).

Thinking patterns:

- Worrying about how you come across to others or what they'll think of you.

- Feeling that everyone is observing and evaluating how well you do socially.

- Feeling tongue-tied or worrying that you won't know what to say.

- Being over-sensitive to any sign of negative feedback or rejection (i.e., "I made a joke and everyone only sort of laughed. They all hate me—I know they do.")

- Feeling that being rejected would be a horrible experience that you couldn't handle.

- Seeing yourself negatively, either in a particular social situation (believing you're too quiet and awkward at parties and bad at making small talk), or overall (i.e., feeling you're boring, unlikeable, too weird, etc.)

Physical symptoms:

- Symptoms of anxiety such as trembling, sweating, an upset stomach, or a racing heart. [xii]

- Physical signs of anxiety or embarrassment you don't want people to notice, such as blushing, sweaty palms, or a tight, constricted voice.

Emotions:

- Embarrassment

- Anxiety

- Guilt

- Shame

Additionally, shyness can be thought of as a temporary state ("I felt shy at that party") or a more global trait ("I'm a shy person.")

Degrees of shyness - Lots of people will tell you they're shy, but they can mean very different things when they say it.

Least Shy:

- People who are generally confident and charismatic in most situations, but they feel shy in the sense that if walk into a room full of strangers, they may feel out of their element for a minute or two before they dive in and start working the crowd.

- People who have it together on the surface, but they're inwardly self-conscious and hesitant at times. They say they feel shy, but it doesn't have much of a practical effect on their lives.

- People who do fine in most social situations, but feel ill at ease in a few of them. For example, they may get really nervous and self-conscious at parties, or networking events, but be fine around their good friends and co-workers.

- People who are shy all around, though not to an extreme degree. Certain scenarios give them the most trouble, but even day to day they're a bit more tongue-tied and uncomfortable around others than average. They have more social insecurities as well. On the whole their shyness doesn't get too in the way of their functioning. It's more of an inconvenience.

- People who act very shy in most social situations, are buried under a mountain of worries, and whose lives are noticeably worse off because of it. If their shyness is severe enough they could have a condition such as social anxiety disorder. xiii, xxx

Most Shy:

- **Coping with shyness** - Some people want every trace of their shyness eliminated. Others see their shyness more as part of their personality and don't necessarily want to completely get rid of it. They may realize they're quiet or inhibited sometimes, but are comfortable with that side of themselves. They may want to be able to handle certain situations better, but have no need to change the fact that they're not total social butterflies at house parties. For someone in the second camp, it can help to take the time to think about what facets of your shyness you want to work on and which ones you're fine to leave as is. It can also be useful to realize and accept that it's okay to remain shy in some ways.

- **Handle insecure thoughts** - Shy people have all kinds of worries and insecurities. These fears are often exaggerated or distorted, but shy people act as if they're realistic, and this prevents them from getting involved in more social situations. If they can control these thoughts they can become more comfortable around people.

- **Try to increase your sense of self-worth and confidence** - Some approaches are about going after negative thoughts directly. Another angle is to try to boost your sense of self-confidence or self-worth. The idea here is that if a person feels good about themselves that will help override any negative or insecure thinking she may have. [xxxiii]

- **Expose yourself to the situations that make you shy** - This is probably the most effective way to overcome shyness in the long term. If certain situations make you feel shy, put yourself in them until you're used to them, and you learn how to act more effectively in them. This is a long, sometimes hard process. Facing your fears is uncomfortable. So is making mistakes and learning from them. Ditto for occasionally getting rejected and learning firsthand that you can handle it.

- **Improve your social skills** - This point won't apply to everyone. Some people who are shy have perfectly good social skills. [vi] Their problem is that their shyness and anxiety prevents those adequate skills from coming out. When they're not feeling too shy, they do just fine in interpersonal situations. Others have underdeveloped people skills in addition to their shyness. On top of learning to handle their inhibited/anxious/insecure symptoms, they could also benefit from learning things such as better ways to make conversation or how to mingle at a party. They'd then need to put in the time to practice and develop those new skills. Although, sometimes just knowing how to handle a social situation can make someone feel more confident in tackling it.

Lighten Up

One broad way to be more socially successful with people is to lighten up a bit. For some people with social difficulties, a core issue they have is that some of their behaviors and attitudes are too uptight. For example:

- They get irritated by social annoyances that most people let slide.

- They care too much about whether or not people are acting in ways they view as inconsiderate and thoughtless.

- They look down on what they see as silly, immature behavior.

- They think they always have to be controlled, proper and well-behaved. They have trouble letting loose and enjoying themselves.

At the heart of uptightness are traits such as:

- Having rigid, unrealistic standards about how you and other people should act, and how the social world should be.

- Not being able to relax and ease up on those standards.

- Being too sensitive to little irritations from the social world, and in people's breaches of your standards.

- Being too touchy and tending to overreact when things do go wrong.

Being uptight is one of those mistakes where just being made aware of it, and being told not to do it, can help—so try to loosen up. Don't get too upset by little things that go wrong when you're around people. [xii, xxxiii] It's also smart to have a realistic idea of what to expect in social situations

There are lots of slightly irritating, but common and unavoidable behaviors and events that come up in social situations. [xxxii] A friend may be unreliable about showing up to a get together. A group of friends may all start interrupting and talking over each other during dinner. A party may be overcrowded and full of sloppy guests who keep jostling you. Most people know these types of things just come with the territory and don't let themselves be too bothered by them.

If you're more socially inexperienced, however, the same things can really irk you. You haven't been around enough to know they're not supposed to be a big deal. In your mind, you may have the expectation that a social situation should and can go a certain way, and then feel upset when people "ruin" it. The thing is, in practice that situation may never have had the potential to turn out the ideal way you pictured it. For example, if you believe you should be able to have an in-depth conversation at a club, you'll always get peeved that it's too loud to do so. If you accept that's just not possible or part of that experience, you'll have a better time. Just like someone shouldn't get bent out of shape for not being able to go nuts and party at a library.

- **Don't take yourself too seriously** - Uptight people often see themselves as refined, intelligent adults who are above the silliness average people engage in. They'll think they're more mature than their peers, and look down on their antics. They think they have to come across as contained and in control at all times. Actually, it's okay to be a normal silly human. [xix] You can watch dumb movies with your friends while gossiping and making crude jokes. You won't lose your Intellectual card. No one will care. In fact they'll probably appreciate it. No one's keeping track of whether you're always acting sophisticated.

There's nothing wrong with light, brainless fun

Uptight people often don't have a very high opinion of anything entertaining, mindless, or pointless. They think it's beneath them, and that they have to be serious all the time. Being serious has its place, but there's nothing wrong with having a good time, either. Having fun just feels good. There's nothing more to it, and that's fine. Not every conversation has to be about reversing global warming.

- Don't be too zealous about following the rules - Uptight people care a bit too much about obeying the rules, and they think other everyone else should too. They can be overly stringent about following them and can get really irritated on general principle when others inevitably don't do everything they're told.

The rules they care about could be explicit laws, like not driving drunk. There could also be general social guidelines they've decided are important, and which they think everyone should never deviate from (i.e., don't talk loudly at a restaurant). Finally, there could be more abstract principles that they expect other people to follow too closely, like thinking everyone should be thoughtful and considerate. In a broader sense, they want everyone to act perfectly, and they get upset when that doesn't happen.

It helps to make peace with the fact that in practice most people don't follow smaller rules to the letter or obey them 100% of the time. [xxxiv] They bend and selectively ignore them. If they don't get caught or hurt anyone, what does it matter? The effect following a rule or not will have on everyone's good time often comes into the equation. An uptight person who rigidly thinks people should never jaywalk, or should always be completely polite and urbane, will eventually make herself crazy.

- **Don't overreact to certain activities** - There are certain social activities uptight people often get annoyed about. Anything that involves people acting loud, stupid, and immature will probably do it. What also gets them is anything with an aura of rule-breaking, danger, or sketchiness around it. So this can include anything involving partying or recklessness, basically.

They dislike faux-dangerous things because their uptight world view gives them a tendency to see things as more sketchy than they actually are. For instance, they may see drinking as a horrible thing to do, when 95% of the time nothing much happens when people do it. Or they may see something like skateboarding as a hobby where young punks are constantly causing trouble or cracking their heads open.

- **Accept the fact that you can't control everything** - This doesn't applies to everyone, but at the root of some people's uptightness is a need to be in control and have everyone act the way they want them to. If you can let this need go, and just accept that people are often going to behave in a way you may not like or expect, it can do a lot to help you adopt a more relaxed mentality. [xxxii]

Chapter 12

SOCIAL SKILLS FOR RELATIONSHIP AND EXPANDING YOUR SOCIAL LIFE

Everyone has relationships, and many people want to expand their social life. The relationships that are the most important to us usually require effort to maintain to keep them healthy and meaningful.

No matter what you want to improve or maintain, communication and social competence is involved. Social competence is a term used by social psychologists to describe the ability to use social skills to interact with others in an effective and healthy manner. [vii, x]

Maintaining Important Relationships

When you've reached a point in a relationship where you know you want to keep it, grow it and stay in it, what do you do? You already know you like each other and that you have fun together; now you have to see whether you can make it work at a higher level. This can be scary because you may not be certain your feelings will be 100% reciprocated; you need to make yourself vulnerable, which means you can be hurt.

Here are some signs that your relationship is ready for the next level:

- **You know her likes and dislikes** – This is a strong indication that you know each other well. Knowing someone well and wanting to be in a long-term relationship with her is a positive sign.

- **You've talked about the future** – This is also an indicator of knowing someone well. You have an idea about how she envisions her future, and you want to be there—that's a thumbs up.

- **Your values are compatible** – The fact is that opposites really don't attract, so having compatible values is a big plus.

- **You know how she'll react in most situations** – Another strong sign that you know her well.

- **You can't imagine being without her** – This doesn't need an explanation, does it?

- **Her happiness is a primary concern of yours** – When you feel this way, you're really there. Now it's time to take the leap and make sure she feels the same way. (You probably didn't get to this point if she doesn't care about you.) This is when you'll be vulnerable, but the old saying applies here: nothing ventured, nothing gained.

Expanding Your Social Circle through Social Skills

In general, people's number one fear is public speaking, followed very closely by the other number one fear: death. That means that people would rather find the answer to the ultimate question rather than speak in front of strangers. Fortunately, being successful in social situations, however, doesn't necessarily have anything to do with speaking.

Here are some ways you can improve your social skills to expand your social circle without having to say a word in a social gathering.

- **Make yourself approachable:** Making yourself approachable really comes down to two important elements: body language and facial expression. People are going to decide whether they want to approach you before they've heard you say a word. So here's how you can say a lot without saying a thing.

- **Body language** - Your body language speaks volumes about you. Next time you're at a social gathering, take a second to think about what you're body language is saying to others. Are you standing against a wall? If so, you could be non-verbally saying: "Please don't bother me, I wish I weren't here." Are your arms folded against your chest? If so, you may be sending out this signal: "Stay away from me, I'm not interested in interacting and I'll rebuff you if you come over." [xiii, xxxix]

The way you stand at a social gathering sends a message to other guests. If you want to send a warm, welcoming message your body language should reflect that desire; this means standing with others, not off on your own. You don't have to be the center of attention, but if you're part of the action, people are more likely to involve you in their conversation. Stand openly even if you aren't comfortable, because you don't have to appear that way. A relaxed, open stance invites other people to enter your space.

Facial expressions: Your face is the gateway to how you feel. This is why a strong poker face can mean the difference between winning the pot, so to speak, or losing it all. You don't necessarily need to bluff in a social setting to win people's interest, but keep in mind that your face is the first thing people see, so what do you want it to say? A friendly smile, an understanding nod, a hearty laugh, and making eye contact are very important. Those things tell others that you are a good audience and someone who is enjoyable to talk to. If you notice yourself rolling your eyes and furrowing your brow in social situations, think about what you're saying to others and why it could be a barrier to achieving social success.

Improve your conversational skills

Most people think that being a good conversationalist has everything to do with speaking confidently on a wide variety of subjects. But before you spend a lot of time studying the latest trends in reality television shows, remember that a conversation has two roles: a speaker and a listener. You don't have to be a renaissance man to be a great conversationalist; you actually don't have to speak much at all.

Actively listen: Active listening is a skill. It means maintaining eye contact and nodding as you listen. It is important that you give a speaker signs that what they're speaking about is reaching you, and that you are interested. This gives them the go ahead to keep talking to you. On the other hand, nodding your head and maintaining eye contact alone are not to show you are engaged in the conversation. Acknowledge that you understand what the person is trying to communicate. This can be cone by the simple repetition of the point they were making, or by restating it. [xxxvi]

Respond to the speaker: If someone has engaged you in a conversation it is probably on a topic that they are interested in. Make sure you ask exploratory questions, which are questions that do *not* yield a yes or no response — they are open-ended. Exploratory or open-ended questions, prompt someone to elaborate. For example, "Can you describe what it's like?" or, "Tell me what happened when..." or "What's your opinion on...?" Those are all questions that can't be answered with a monosyllabic response and will yield further insight into a person, a topic or provide the necessary material to allow a natural conversational progression to a new topic.

Finally, respond to the speaker. People want to hear your own thoughts and opinions. Responding with your own ideas or opinions— after you've taken the time to understand the speaker's perspective—can change you from a nodding, robotic yes-man into an independent thinker who is interested in what the other person has to say.

Recognize and Adapt to Social Norms

Any social setting is just small society with its own norms, values and standards. For example, a nightclub social setting values different things than the setting for a public book reading. Understand what a social setting's norms are and how you can conform to them. It is important to understand your audience if you value being successful in social situations, because if you don't understand your audience, you will just end up alienating yourself and others.

Dressing for success in a social situation: Going to a club in jeans and a T-shirt would be inappropriate and start you off on the wrong foot. Dressing for social success means that you show up in attire that is appropriate for the occasion and the environment. To ensure you are dressing appropriately for an event, you can call other people that you may be going with and ask them what they will be wearing. After all, asking ahead of time is much better than wishing you had after it's too late. [vii]

Know the lingo: Understand your social setting and what is appropriate to talk about. Most people think it's generally safe to stay away from topics such as politics and religion. Depending on your audience, however, you may need to consider other topics to avoid. For example, while at a bachelor party, don't talk about your recent divorce or how you love the single lifestyle. Just like different cultures have different dialects, so do different social settings. It is important to know the dialect that is appropriate to your social setting, and that means think before you speak (which is always a good idea, no matter what). Even if you don't intend to be offensive, if someone takes offense from how you conduct yourself, it's already too late.

Be a social butterfly - Most of the tips above can be practiced in a variety of situations. You can be an active listener in any conversation. The same can be said about your body language, facial expressions and general behavior. Practice in environments where you are already comfortable. You can do this at work, among friends or with family. It is important to get a better handle on the process of nonverbal communication ahead of social situations rather than using social situations as an experiment.

Ultimately, the goal is to make you feel more confident in social situations. To achieve that confidence requires practice; if you practice you will improve your nonverbal skills and this will prepare you for any social setting. Once you are prepared, you will feel confident; when you're confident, you will feel comfortable; when you're comfortable, you're more likely to be yourself. None of this is dependent on being the center of attention or the life of a party. Rather, it is dependent on being a good communicator who understands who they're talking to. And don't forget a large part of the learning curve: observe, observe, observe. [xxxiii, xxxvi]

Building and Sustaining Relationships

There are so many things that could go on a list of important skills to develop when building or establishing a relationship. Some behavioral psychologists agree that there is one single social skill that is the **most important of all: the art of listening.** [xxxvi]

People come to see a counselor with a problem they don't know how to handle; they sit down with a defeated, hopeless air, and they begin to talk. They talk, the counselor listens. Often they stand up at the end of the session with a very different attitude. "Thank you so much. I feel so much better," they say. Counselors report they may have only spoken a couple of sentences the entire time, but just having someone who was interested in their problem did the most good. Just having someone willing to listen is all that most people need. Finding someone who will listen, *really listen*, is a rare skill these days. Few people know how to turn the mouth off and the ears on. There's more to listening than merely hearing what someone is saying. If everyone would practice these listening skills, there would be fewer problems in the world

Look people in the eye - How many times have you tried to talk to someone who was looking somewhere else? It's frustrating isn't it?

We often demand that our children look at us when we talk to them, because if we can't see the eyes, we feel they aren't listening. Look someone in the eye when he's talking to you. Give him your undivided attention. It'll do wonders for how people perceive you.

Look interested - Nod at the appropriate time, or shake your head when it is called for. Add a helpful, "Wow," or "That's interesting," or "I'm so sorry," here and there. Make sure that your facial expression reflects the fact that you are listening. Don't stare off into the distance, fiddle with your fingers, or tap your foot impatiently. Look patient and interested. Give them your full ear and attention.

Ask small, clarifying questions - This is important. When someone is talking, interrupt only to ask small, clarifying questions that demonstrate your willingness to listen to them. Doing this also accomplishes two other very important things. First, it shows them that you care. People who don't care, don't bother to ask questions. When someone cares for you they inquire after your health, ask about your family, or ask your opinion on something. People always gravitate to someone who cares enough to ask important clarifying questions.

Secondly, it steers the conversation toward the best resolution. When someone is hurting, excited, or struggling they often can't see the problem clearly. Since you don't have as much at stake emotionally in whatever issue is on the table, you will probably see it better than they do. That being the case, your questions can gently steer them toward the obvious resolution.

Most people intrinsically know what needs to be done with a problem. But while under the emotional stress of the problem, they can become paralyzed or befuddled in their thinking. Asking clarifying questions helps steer them to what they know they should do. Counselors report that patients often arrive at the best answer themselves when given the opportunity to talk to an active, understanding listener.

The art of listening is an essential skill for anyone who wants to help build their relationships, endear people to them, and foster trust between two people. A good listener makes people feel secure, loved, cared for, and accepted. Give it a try. You'll like it.

Building Communication Skills in Important Relationships

Most people have important relationships in their lives. These are often family or marital relationships, but they can be friendships or any number of other highly valued relationships that take time to forge and maintain¯and are worth all the effort we put into them. [xxxvii] Communication in these friendships, fellowships or alliances is a two-way street; often what we give we get back.

In a significant relationship like a marriage, when husband and wife cannot communicate, a huge dam is built that stops the flow of water. This causes everything around them to suffer. Seeds that were once planted stop growing and both spouses develop unmet needs, eventually causing damage in the relationship. Many promising marriages have fallen apart simply because of a lack of communication.

Communication Breakdowns

Although we speak with people every day, true communication is a more personal and dynamic event that is critical for growth in relationships. Men and women inherently communicate differently, so it should be no surprise when communication challenges arise between couples. Since effective communication is essential to moving ahead in life, when there are problems relating to each other, it can cause problems in any relationship.

There are thousands of books written on this topic alone. Communication is a huge topic, and while we may all understand what the word means, we often completely fail to understand its process and power to influence radical change in all areas of life. [xxxv] By itself, communication alone ends many marriages. Both spouses may love each, but without proper communication, that love can go unnoticed and the result is sometimes unnecessarily sad.

Understand, Not Understood

Communication failure occurs when one person feels that he or she is not understood. How many times do you react when a loved one doesn't understand you? We want to be understood, we want to know that our husband or wife, friend, or loved one understands us. And when we don't feel understood, we react, whether silently, verbally, or with action. Usually those reactions are negative, and they feed into the cycle of breakdown. But consider this: of all the times you focused on not being understood, how often have you tried to understand the other person? It often doesn't occur to us in an argument that our partner is also trying to be understood just like us. If we sought to understand more, rather than always seeking to be understood, a lot of arguing would cease and we might find that the cycle of unnecessary hurt is broken. [xviii]

The Problem of Arguing and Failed Communication

When we're awake, we spend approximately 70% our time communicating, 30% of which is talking. This means that over half of our communication is non-verbal. [xxxv] So it's not what you say, it's how you say it that can be the cause of communication problems between most people. If you say one thing for instance, such as "everything is fine" but your body language conveys something else, such as sunken shoulders or a withdrawn face, the dominant communication will be the physical undertone. When communication between couples is strained or even nonexistent, the entire foundation of the relationship is affected.

Learning to communicate so everyone involved feels heard is hard work, and as the divorce rate shows, many couples are unable to reach this level of understanding and therefore issues are left unresolved as tension grows, leading to a lack of understanding and respect. Ultimately, this could lead to couples simply dissolving the relationship for lack of knowing how to fix the problems. Unfortunately, the same problems could also arise in subsequent relationships. Communicating effectively is an art but it can be learned by almost everyone.

Why Is Communicating So Difficult?

For the most part, communication breaks down when people fail to adequately say what and how they feel in a non-threatening manner. If we were all completely honest, which of course means making ourselves vulnerable, the majority of arguments and conflicts would not occur.

As children, we go through experiences, good and bad, that ultimately affect how we communicate in the future. The term "emotional baggage" is used to describe these feelings we carry forward. If, for example, you grew up in a household with an angry parent that everyone constantly tried to avoid or soothe, you will likely carry this attitude into adulthood and when confrontation arises, whether real or perceived, you will either try to calm the situation or run from it. [xx, xxiii] If your spouse says something you perceive to be angry or threatening, you may revert back to this childhood memory and in turn, face your mate with your learned response. You will probably do whatever you can to avoid the subject and if your spouse, for instance, comes from a family where everyone accepts anger as a simple outpouring of emotion and nothing more, then the two of you may clash, making resolution of issues a regular challenge.

Countless books on the subject of gender communication have concluded that men and women think and feel differently. Men communicate in order to relay information. In general, they tend to talk more about topics and do not require discussions relating to feelings and emotions. Men are competitive problem solvers. They will often talk to solve problems. Conversely, women typically communicate to connect with others. They would rather talk about people than things and they relay feelings quite readily. Women are more relationship-oriented in their speech then men. These differences provide a challenge for us to relate effectively to each other. [xxxii, xxxiv]

Going into a relationship, we often have unrealistic expectations. Romantic novels and blockbuster movies with the smart, beautiful heroine finally getting her perfect, sympathetic man are not like the real world. When we are shocked back to reality during our first communication breakdown, we feel cheated, disappointed, and often angry. Hurt feelings lead to irrational behavior and blaming, which of course, lead to further communication problems and eventual relationship troubles.

Effective Communication is a Skill

Communicating effectively with each other in a relationship does not usually come naturally. It may seem that way in the beginning, but as most couples know, once the honeymoon phase is over, the real challenge begins. A joint commitment to build communication is necessary to build greater understanding. This is a skill, and you will need to practice it in of life, probably many times, but the good news is that anyone can learn it.

How to Recognize When You Need Help

Communication problems are like little ticking time bombs. You never know what will set things off and when it will be "the last straw" for either party. There are early warning signs that a relationship in is trouble however. If two people have consistent unresolved arguments, if either of you is unhappy most of the time or you find you are no longer doing things together, you should seek outside. If you no longer feel "in love" with your mate, or you are contemplating an affair, this is a sign there is trouble in the marriage. If you are constantly tired, depressed, distracted at work, or you just feel like you argue about everything, counseling can often help.

The sooner you address these communications problems, the better off your relationship will be, offering each of you the opportunity to have your needs met in the relationship. Effective communication is not something most people automatically know how to do; it's a skill people have to learn. xxxv

Building Effective Communication Skills

Learning good communication skills provides lasting ways build healthier relationships. Here are some of the basic and most important ones:

- Speak in terms of how you feel; don't accuse the other party. Example: "I feel hurt when you don't want to talk about our problems," is better than "You never listen to anything I say."

- Stay calm. Keep your voice at a speaking level and control your anger. This is one of the most important keys to good communication under stress.
- Keep things in perspective; be sure to recognize the good parts in the relationship. If necessary, enumerate the things that attracted you to each other in the beginning. [xv, xxxiv]
- Acknowledge the feelings of the other party. Communication is a two-way street. Your spouse or friend isn't enjoying the conflict any more than you are.

Habits of People Who Build Extraordinary Relationships

Important relationships worth developing and keeping aren't always personal ones. Professional and business relationships can be worth a lifetime of good business—not to mention profits. However, good business relationship principles can usually transition in our personal lives as well. The most extraordinary professional relationships are built by ordinary, thoughtful actions. One fact is universal: real success, the kind that exists on multiple levels, is impossible without building great relationships. Real success is impossible unless you treat other people with kindness, regard, and respect. That's why people who build extraordinary business relationships:

Take the hit - A customer gets mad. A vendor complains about poor service. A mutual friend feels slighted. Sometimes, whatever the issue and regardless of who is actually at fault, some people step in and take the hit. They're willing to accept the criticism because they know they can handle it—they don't take it personally. [xxxiv] Few acts are more effective than taking the undeserved hit. And few acts better cement a relationship.

Step in without being asked - It's easy to help when you're asked. Most people will to it. Very few people offer help *before* they have been asked, even though most of the time that is when a little help will make the greatest impact. People who build extraordinary relationships pay close attention so they can tell when others are struggling. Then they offer to help, but not in a general, "Is there something I can do to help you?" way. Instead they come up with specific ways they can help. That way they can push past the reflexive response of, "No, I'm okay" rejections. And they roll up their sleeves and make a difference in another person's life, not because they want to build a better relationship, although that is certainly the result, but because they really care.

Answer the question that isn't asked - Where relationships are concerned, often people will ask a different question than the one they really want answered. A colleague might ask you whether he should teach a class at a local college, when he really wants to talk about how to take his life in a different direction. A partner might ask how you felt about the idea he presented during the last board meeting, when he really wants to talk about his diminished role in running of company. An employee might ask how you built a successful business; instead of kissing up he might be looking for some advice—and encouragement—to help him follow his own dreams.

Behind many simple questions is often a larger question that goes unasked. People who build great relationships think about what lies underneath so they can answer that question, too.

Know when to dial it back - Outgoing and charismatic people are usually a lot of fun—until they aren't. When a major challenge pops up or a situation gets stressful, some people can't stop "expressing their individuality." (Most of us know at least one person so enamored of his personality he can *never* dial it back.) People who build great relationships know when to have fun and when to be serious, when to be over the top and when to be invisible, and when to take charge and when to follow. Great relationships are multifaceted and therefore require multifaceted people willing to adapt to the situation, and to the people in that situation. [xxiii]

Prove they think of others - People who build great relationships don't just think about other people. They act on those thoughts. One easy way is to give unexpected praise. Everyone loves unexpected praise—it's like getting flowers not because it's Valentine's Day, but "just because." Praise helps others feel better about themselves and lets them know you're thinking about them (which, if you think about it, is flattering in itself.) Take a little time every day to do something nice for someone you know, not because you're expected to, but simply because you can. When you do, your relationships improve dramatically.

Realize when people have acted poorly - Most people apologize when their actions or words are called into question. Very few people apologize before they are asked to—or even before anyone notices they should. Responsibility is a key building block of a great relationship. People who take the blame, who say they are sorry and explain why they are sorry, who don't try to push any of the blame back on the other person, are people everyone wants in their lives, because they instantly turn a mistake into a bump in the road rather than a permanent roadblock.

Give consistently, receive occasionally - A great relationship is mutually beneficial. In business terms that means connecting with people who can be mentors, who can share information, and help create other connections. In short, that means going into a relationship wanting *something*. The person who builds great relationships doesn't think about what she wants; she starts by thinking about what she can give. She sees giving as the best way to establish a real relationship and a lasting connection. She approaches building relationships as if it's all about the other person and not about her, and in the process she builds relationships with people who follow the same approach. Over time, they make real lasting connections, and real friends.

Value the message by always valuing the messenger - When someone speaks from a position of position of power or authority, it's tempting to place greater emphasis on their input, advice, and ideas. But how about the guy who mows our lawn? Maybe we don't listen to him so much. That's unfortunate. Smart people strip away the framing that comes with the source—whether positive or negative—and consider the information, advice, or idea based solely on its merits.

People who build great relationships never automatically discount the message simply because they discount the messenger. They know good advice is good advice, regardless of where it comes from, and they know good people are good people, regardless of their perceived status.

Start small, and be happy to stay small – Once a guy who often wears a Reading Football Club sweatshirt was out shopping. The checkout clerk at the grocery store noticed it one day and said, "Oh, you're a Reading supporter? My team is Manchester United." The guy—normally shy—responded, "You think Man U can beat Real Madrid next week?" The clerk grinned and said, "Oh yeah. We'll crush them!" Although it didn't turn out that way, now, whenever they're in the store at the same time, the clerk waves, often from across the store. The other guy almost always walk over to say hi, and they talk briefly about soccer.

That's as far as that relationship is likely to go and that's okay. For a couple of minutes they step outside the customer/employee relationship and become two people brightening each other's day.

And that's enough, because every relationship, however minor and possibly fleeting, has value. People who build great relationships treat every one of their relationships that way. That's a lesson most of us need to take to heart more often. [xxxii]

CONCLUSION

Social skills are learned and practiced from the moment we're born.

Some of us learn them more easily than others, but when we utilize them, they make it easier to get alone in the world.

The world today is changing faster than we seem to be able to keep up with it. There are more people in it, and different kinds of people, too. We have to adapt to many challenges, but good social skills evolve and assist us there, too.

We can learn to improve our skills, and we use them everywhere we go, at work, to school, and on outings with friends. Some physiological conditions like autism and Asperger Syndrome make learning them more difficult, but there are specialists, programs and organizations designed to assist in those cases.

Social skills and relationships require working at, but curiously, doing them well boils down to being very close to what many of us heard our mothers say when we were young: "Do the nicest possible thing in the nicest possible way."

Bibliography

[i] U.S. Interim Projections by Age, Sex, Race and Hispanic Origin. Washington, DC: U.S. Census Bureau; 2004. Available at: http://www.census.gov/ipc/www/usinterimproj. July 13, 2006.

[ii] Ahlenius, Hugo. "Trends in population, developed and developing countries, 1750-2050 (estimates and projections.)" The Environmental Food Crisis - The Environment's Role in Averting Future Food Crises, 2009.

[iii] Kotkin, Joel and Mark Schill. "A Map of America's Future: Where Growth Will Be over the Next Decade". Forbes. (04 September 2013. Published 23, September 2013, Forbes Issue. Online 12 January 2014). www.forbes.com/sites/joelkotkin/2013/09/04/a-map-of-americas-future-where-growth-will-be-over-the-next-decade/

[iv] "Culture Shock." Study Abroad Center, U of Ca-Irvine. (Website) www.cie.uci.edu/prepare/shock.html

[v] Bond, Michael Harris, Peter B. Smith and Ciğdem Kağitçibasi. "Understanding Social Psychology across Cultures: Living and

Working with Others in a Changing World." Some Pressing Questions for Cross-Cultural Psychology Ch.1. (Ver.16.May. Online 10 January 2014).

www.sagepub.com/upm-data/9862_039473Ch.1pdf

vi Tajfel, Henri. *Human Groups and Social Categories: Studies in Social Psychology*. Press Syndicate of the University of Cambridge. New York, 2010.

vii Kennedy-Moore, Ph.D., Eileen. "What are Social Skills? Helping Children Become Comfortable and Competent in Social Situations." *Growing Friendships*, August 18, 2011.

viii Young, Scott. "You Won't Get Anywhere with Poor Social Skills." Pick the Brain (blog 2008). 5 January 2014.

http://www.pickthebrain.com/blog/social-skills

ix Ladd, G. W. (1990). "Having Friends, Keeping Friends, Making Friends, and Being Liked by Peers in the Classroom: Predictors of Children's Early School Adjustment?" *Child Development*, 6 1, 312-331.

x Albrecht, Karl. Social Intelligence: The New Science of Success; Beyond IQ, Beyond EI,   Applying Multiple Intelligence

Theory to Human Interaction. Jossey-Bass 2006.

www.karlalbrecht.com

xi Bennis, Warren Professor. "Foreword." Social Intelligence: The New Science of Success; Beyond IQ, Beyond EI, Applying Multiple Intelligence Theory to Human Interaction.   Jossey-Bass 2006. (Online eBook 18 January 2014). www.josseybass.com.

xii "Social Skills/Social Awareness." Special Education Service Agency. www.sese.org/content/autism-impairment/Social-Skills-Strategies

xiii Bennington-Castro, Joseph. "The Science of What Makes an Introvert and an Extrovert."
The Daily Explainer, September 10, 2013.

xiv Morgan, J.P. Introversion-Extroversion. Psychological Bulletin, Vol 31 (5), May 1934.

xv Lieberman, M., "Why We Are Wired to Connect." Scientific American, October 13, 2013.

xvi Cacioppo, J., et al. "Loneliness affects how the brain operates." (2009, Feb. 19) Science Daily Found online at
http://www.sciencedaily.com/releases/2009/02/090215151800

[xvii] Brehm, S. S. and Kassin, S. M. (1996). *Social Psychology* 3rd Ed. Boston: Houghton Mifflin Company.

[xviii] Smith, E.R. "Socially Situated Cognition: Cognition in its Social Context." *Advances in Experimental Social Psychology*, Vol. 36. Pp 52-117, 2012.

[xix] Mize, J., & Pettit, G. S. (1994, July). "From Parent Coaching to Peer Acceptance: Behavioral and Social Cognitive Mediators." In J. Mize & M. Dekovic (Co-chairs), *Mechanisms in the Transmission of Social Competence*. Symposium presented at the International Society for the Study of Behavioral Development, Amsterdam.

[xx] Weisenfeld, Esther. "The Concept of "We": A Community Social Psychology Myth?" Journal of Community Psychology, Vol. 24, Issue 4, pp 337-346, 2001.

[xxi] "Peer Socialization in School". The Association for Supervision and Curriculum Development. (1969) (Online 22 January 2014).

[xxii] National Dissemination Center for Children with Disabilities U.S. Dept. of Education, Office of Special Education Programs 1825 Connecticut Avenue NW, Suite 700 Washington, DC   20009

nichcy@aed.org

http://www.nichcy.org

[xxiii] Social Neuroscience". (Online 18 January 2014).

www.en.wikipedia.org//wiki/Social_neuroscience

[xxiv] "Asperger Syndrome." Medline Plus. U.S. National Library of Medicine and National Institute of Health. 3 January 2014.

http://www.nlm.nih.gov/medlineplus/ency/article/001549.htm

[xxv] Autism, Asperger Syndrome, and PDD, Services for

P.O. Box 524

Crown Point, IN   46308

info@aspergersyndrome.org

http://www.aspergersyndrome.org/

[xxvi] Autism Society of America

4340 East-West Highway

Suite 350

Bethesda, MD   20814

http://www.autism-society.org

[xxvii] "Autistic Spectrum Disorders". NHS Choices Your Health Your Choices (February 2012). 5 January 2014.

www.nhs.uk/conditions/autistic-spectrum-
disorder/Pages/Introduction.aspx

xxviii *Mantel, Ruth. "Must Have Job Skills in 2013." The Wall Street Journal. N.p., 18 Nov. 2012. Web. 20 Apr. 2013.*

xxix Fox, Marcia G., Ph.D. and Leslie Sokol, Ph.D., "Building Unshakeable Confidence." Think Confident, Be Confident for Teens. Ch. 8, pg. 180 (2011, New Harbinger Publications, Inc.)

xxx Shute, N. (2008, Nov. 12). "Why loneliness is bad for your health." *U.S. News and World Report.* Found online at
http://health.usnews.com/articles/health/2008/11/12/why-
loneliness-is-bad-for-your-health.html

xxxi Thomas, A. & Grimes, J. (Eds.) (2002). "Best Practices in School Psychology IV."
Bethesda, MD: The National Association of School Psychologists.

xxxii Diener, E. and Rober-Biswas Diener (2008) *Happiness: Unlocking the Mysteries of Psychological Wealth.* Blackwell: Oxford.

xxxiii Lyubormirsky, Sonja. *The How of Happiness - A Scientific Approach to Getting the Life You Want.* New York: Penguin Press. 2008.

xxxiv Fredrickson, Ph.D., Barbara. *Positivity.* Random House, 2009.

xxxv Shambhala, David Richo. How to Be An Adult in Relationships: the Five Keys to Mindful Loving. (Copyright in paperback May 2002).
http://www.spiritualityandpractice.com/books/books.php?id.5241

xxxvi Baker, Gregory. The Most Important Communication and Social Skill Ever. http://fitlyspoken.org
http://EzineArticles.com/3642815

xxxvii Hamlin, Ph.D., Greg. How to Develop Communication Skills in Marriage: Basic Rules for Couples to Get Started. *Steps for Change*, November 26, 2011.

xxxviii Trunk, Penelope. "Secret Social Skills Successful People Know." How to Blog Office Politics, December 14, 2011.

xxxix Cacioppo, J. (2008, Nov. 3). "How to Cope with Loneliness." *Big Think.* http://bigthink.com/johncacioppo/john-cacioppo-on-how-to-cope-with-loneliness

[xl] U.S. Bureau of the Census (1996). Warmer, older, more diverse:
State-by-state
Population changes to 2025 (PPL-47). Washington, DC: U.S.
Department of
Commerce

[xli] "What is Autism?" The National Autistic Society, 2 January
2014. www.autism.org.uk.

CPSIA information can be obtained at www.ICGtesting.com
Printed in the USA
LVOW12s1532030614

388429LV00020B/1225/P